7 ½' DELUXE BALSAM FIR   6 ½' NEW ENGLAND PINE

The Christmas Tree Book

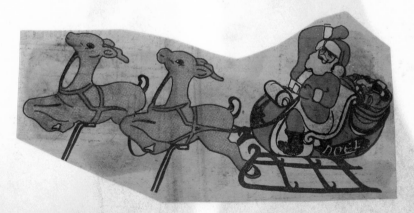

A Studio Book
The Viking Press
New York

The Christmas Tree Book

Phillip V. Snyder

Photographs by Roy Coggin

The History of the
Christmas Tree
and
Antique
Christmas Tree
Ornaments

To the memory of my grandfather,
Leon VanHekle,
who loved Christmas.

And to my parents,
who created for their children
the happiest of Christmases.

First published in 1976 by The Viking Press
625 Madison Avenue, New York, N.Y. 10022
Published simultaneously in Canada by the
Macmillan Company of Canada Limittd

Text and black-and-white illustrations
printed in the United States of America
Color illustrations printed in Japan

Library of Congress Cataloging in Publication Data
Snyder, Phillip V.   1936–
The Christmas tree book. (A Studio book) Bibliography: p.
Includes index.
1. Christmas trees—History. 2. Christmas
decorations—History. 3. Christmas—United States.
I. Coggin, Roy. II. Title.
GT4985.S59   394.2'68282'028   76-40224
ISBN 0-670-22115-5

Contents

Preface and Acknowledgments

One of the nicest things about a Christmas tree is that it looks good no matter how you decorate it.

At the beginning of this century a family of Swedes settled in northern Illinois among Germans. They had never had the Christmas tree tradition and they didn't have much money for ornaments. They hung their silver knives and forks and spoons on the tree.

A few years ago an American couple found themselves living in London without many of their household possessions, including their Christmas tree ornaments. On Christmas Eve they bought a small evergreen at a florist's shop. Back in their flat they improvised by decorating it with his cuff links, and her earrings, bracelets, and bright-colored gloves. When they finished, they decided it was the most beautiful tree they had ever had.

A New York writer decided to give up Christmas trees when she married a man whose Jewish upbringing had precluded them. For several years they had none, although she occasionally told him about her childhood trees. Unexpectedly, one Christmas Eve her husband came home with a little tree over his shoulder. For a few minutes she didn't know how to decorate it. Then she went to her kitchen and found a bunch of marshmallows. She poked holes in the middle and put colored strings through them and tied them all over the tree. They have had a Christmas tree every year since.

One of the most unusual trees of all time was decorated in a New York hotel room during Christmastime in 1897. James Clements, previously a Southern Pacific Railroad brakeman, and his wife decorated an evergreen with seventy thousand dollars' worth of gold nuggets he had found that year in the Klondike gold rush.

In Boston's Post Office Square in the 1920s the SPCA used to erect a horses' Christmas tree. On Christmas Eve the few draft animals remaining in the business district gathered around to nibble apples and sugar lumps from the tree. Pennsylvania farmers similarly put up trees in their barnyards, decorating them with carrots and cabbages and other things animals like to eat.

This book is dedicated to the innocent childlike side of our nature, which perpetuates this happiest of customs.

7

A frontier woman photographer, Friederike Recknagel, took this picture of her husband and daughter with the family tree in Round Top, Texas, in the 1880s.

I am profoundly grateful to two people and an institution, without which this book would not have been possible. The first is Eva Stille, of Frankfurt, Germany, whose *Alter Christbaumschmuck* was, until this book, the only one on the subject of Christmas tree ornaments in the world. The second is Harry Wilson Shuart of Suffern, New York, an ornament collector and dedicated researcher whose scholarship on this subject far exceeds the knowledge of any professional historian or institution I have been able to discover. His articles for *Spinning Wheel* magazine are virtually the only historical material ever to appear in an American magazine about tree ornaments. He graciously shared with me information gathered throughout a lifetime of interest in the subject. The last of my three invaluable sources was the New York Public Library, without which this book would probably never have been started, or much of it made possible. I would like to thank that wonderful institution and its staff for allowing me to, among other things, spend hundreds of hours reading the Christmas issues of *The New York Times* since the newspaper's inception in 1851.

I would like to thank Thomas Congalton of the Shiny-Brite company, who put me in touch with Robert and Harold Eckardt, the sons of Max Eckardt, who founded an ornament company. Shiny-Brite, together with the Corning Glass Company, originated the American ornament business late in the 1930s. Robert and Harold Eckardt provided firsthand knowledge not only of their father and his business, but also of the German village of Lauscha, the town that invented the glass Christmas tree ornament.

I would also like to thank Joseph Ward, retired President of NOMA Lites, who led me to Louis Szel, a pioneer in tree lighting and a man whose personal knowledge of the subject goes back to 1907. Despite his eighty-three years, Szel's memory proved encyclopedic and his correspondence as lively as himself.

I am especially grateful to John Noble, Toy Curator of the Museum of the City of New York. His interest in and knowledge of ornaments was an early inspiration for this book.

Special thanks are in order for Jo Dinslage, a German businessman working in the United States in 1974, for his translation of Eva Stille's book and other German sources for me. I am very grateful to Museum Books of New York for tracing and locating a copy of that out-of-print volume in Germany.

I am indebted to the late Ernst Hartwig of Coburg, Germany,

who provided information as well as several molds used by the ornament makers of Lauscha. I am also grateful to Joachim and Ilse Hartwig, his son and daughter, who introduced me to Harry Eisenwiener, guide and translator for my visit to Lauscha.

I am grateful to Dr. Gerhard Slawinger and his wife, Vroni, who helped me to find and translate information in Germany.

I would like to acknowledge the aid of my friend John Roberson, who read and provided editorial advice and assistance at several stages of my manuscript's development.

I am profoundly grateful to Roy Coggin, the extraordinary photographer who took the beautiful ornament pictures for this book. I am equally grateful to Marcia Higgins, my agent, and to David Bell of Viking, who believed there should be a book on this subject long before he ever saw my manuscript.

While most of the ornaments are from my own collection, I would like to thank Robert Briggs, Leslie Dorsey, and Calvin Jenkins, who very generously allowed us to photograph objects from their outstanding collections.

I am grateful beyond words to my wife, Susan, whose interest, advice, and typing have immeasurably helped me write this book.

And lastly, I'd like to thank the following people, each of whom has contributed in some valuable way to this project: Charlotte Angeletti, Raymond Beecher, Gail C. Belden, Molly Blayney, Barbara Burn, Leah Burt, James Burton, D. J. Carr, James W. Coleman, Jr., Ray Cox, Jean Crowley, Mary Catherine Cutter, Gael Towey Dillon, Leslie Dorsey, Eleanor Eddy, Proctor Ely, Muriel Enslein, Jonathan Fairbanks, Daniel J. Foley, Catherine Lynn Frangiamore, Mauro Fuggetta, Susan Gillias, Stella Grafakos, Dr. Imre D. Gregor, William Hamilton, Otto Hilbert, Elizabeth H. Hill, Christopher Holme, Jane Hoos, Freya Jeschka, Gordon Kibbee, Robert Lindsley, George Malcomson, Kathlene Mandry, Alfred Mayor, Janet McCaffery, Maxwell McCormick, Ernest Morgan, Seymour Moss, L. F. Muehling, Barbara Paone, Robert Pryor, Malcolm A. Rogers, Jr., Christian Rohlfing, Rodris Roth, Robert Roughsedge, Campbell Rutledge, Walter Schatzki, Rene Schumacher, Louis Serrilli, Jeanne Cameron Shanks, Johnston Shimer, J. J. Smith, Frank H. Sommer, Virginia Squair, the late Bohumil Stack, James Still, Allyn Thompson, Robert VanBrundt, Hubert Wilkie, Alice Winchester, Frances Wolf, Terry C. Yates, and Hy Zazula.

I
THE CHRISTMAS TREE'S
FAMILY TREE

here is no existing account of the first Christmas tree. In fact it was not until the sixteenth century that the earliest historical references appeared. Surprisingly enough, the two oldest pieces of documentation are not from Germany, a country associated in most people's minds with the Christmas tree, but from Latvia and Estonia, in what is now the Soviet Union. In the old Baltic port cities of Riga, in 1510, and Reval, in 1514, two tree celebrations were recorded: in each city on Christmas Eve, after a festive dinner, black-hatted members of the local merchants' guild carried an evergreen tree decorated with artificial roses to the market-place, where, in a seeming vestige of paganism, they danced around the tree and then set fire to it.

Nevertheless, it is to Germany that we must look for the development of the Christmas tree tradition. We know, for instance, that in 1531 in Alsace, then a German territory but now part of France, Christmas trees were sold in the Strasbourg market and taken into homes where they were set up undecorated for the holiday. We can assume that this was a common practice, for there was a sixteenth-

11

A German Christmas Eve, 1796.

century forest ordinance passed in Ammerschweier, also in Alsace, stating that no person "shall have for Christmas more than one bush of more than eight shoe lengths." Considering the size of a man's foot in those days, the law thus limited the Christmas tree to little more than four feet in height. Still, the people of Ammerschweier were luckier than many; ordinances in nearby districts forbade the taking of any greens for Christmas.

In spite of the lack of written evidence, we know from our study of primitive cultures that trees remaining green in the winter have long suggested special godlike powers. Prehistoric man would regularly take in green boughs or full evergreen trees at the winter solstice for use in magical rites intended to insure the protection of his home and the return of vegetation to the otherwise brown and dead forest.

As Christianity supplanted older, pagan religions, the decorating of evergreens continued in various parts of northern Europe on many special occasions, including Easter and Midsummer's Day. The Maypole is known to have begun as an evergreen tree and originally bore many of the same decorations that were used on the first Christmas trees. The Roman Catholic Church frequently banned or otherwise tried to discourage the use of the evergreen, but the age-old custom remained so deeply ingrained in the German culture that the tree eventually became transformed into a Christian symbol.

Although the veneration of the evergreen is firmly rooted in pre-Christian traditions, the Christmas tree has two interesting Christian traditions behind it. During the fourteenth and fifteenth centuries evergreens with apples hung from their boughs were known to have played an important role in the miracle plays presented in or outside churches on the twenty-fourth of December. Since few people could read the Scripture, miracle plays dramatized stories from the Bible as a way of teaching the congregation. In the early church calendar of saints December 24 was Adam and Eve's Day, the occasion for a play depicting the dramatic events concerning the fruit tree in the Garden of Eden. In many cities, before the performance the actors paraded through the streets with the actor who would portray Adam carrying the "Paradise tree." In place of the winter-bare branches of a real apple tree, an evergreen decorated with apples was the usual substitute. Since this tree was the only prop on the stage during the play, the image left a lasting impression associated with Christmas long after the medieval miracle plays were no longer performed. By the seventeenth century evergreens hung with apples were no longer considered strictly trees of temptation and were traditionally decorated each Christmas, though as late as the latter part of the nineteenth century people in northern Germany still bought little figures of Adam and Eve and the serpent to put under their "Tree of Life."

The Christmas tree also has Christian associations as old as the tenth century that link it to flowering or fruit-bearing trees rather than to the evergreen. Throughout Europe there are records and folk tales concerning trees and bushes that mysteriously burst into bloom on Christmas Eve or Day. Beginning in the sixteenth century references indicate that many Germans cut cherry and other flowering branches and took them into their homes on St. Andrew's Day (November 30). The branches were put in water in a warm room and "forced" in the hope of obtaining blooms in time for Christmas.

The oldest Christmas tree to be decorated standing in a parlor as we know the tradition today is described in a fragment of a 1605 travel diary left us by an unidentified visitor to Strasbourg. The writer tells of fir trees set up and hung with paper roses of many different colors and with apples, flat wafers, gilded candies, and sugar. In early Christian art the rose was a symbol for the Virgin Mary, and the flat wafers are obviously related to the "host," the communion symbol for Christ. A tree decorated with such wafers or cookies with religious designs became known as a *Christbaum*. By the seventeenth century, then, the age-old, winter-defying evergreen was a common sight in Christian homes honoring the Christ Child each Christmas. Interestingly enough, a museum in Munich has in its collection several small geometric and floral Christmas tree decorations, made from pastel-tinted host wafers by an old woman who remembers similar versions still in use in Bavaria during the first years of the twentieth century.

Throughout the seventeenth and eighteenth centuries the *Christbaum* appeared in a number of different forms. In parts of Austria and Germany, the tip was cut from a large evergreen and hung upside down in the corner of the living room and sometimes decorated with strips of red paper, apples, and gilded nuts. Others were hung in windows or from the rafters of a room, tip upward, with the butt sharpened and an apple hanging from the point. As late as the nineteenth century, decorated trees hung upside down over the doors of some German homes.

The oldest description of a tree decorated with candles comes from a sister-in-law of Louis XIV of France. In a letter written in 1708, Liselotte von der Pfalz, who was born in 1652, described Christmas trees as she remembered them from her own German childhood. "Tables are fixed up like altars and outfitted for each child with all sorts of things, such as new clothes, silver, dolls, sugar candy, and so forth. Boxwood trees are set on the tables, and a candle is fastened to each branch."

The *Christbaum*'s growing popularity was not always endorsed by the Church. Johann Konrad Dannahauer, a theologian from Strasbourg, attacked the new habit in the 1640s, writing, "Among other trifles which are set up during Christmas time instead of God's word is the Christmas tree or fir tree which is put up at home and decorated with dolls and sugar."

At about the same time that the use of evergreens for Christmas trees was becoming popular, a Christmas tree–like decoration called a "pyramid" also came into use. Cut evergreen boughs were wrapped around open pyramid-shaped wooden frames, which were then decorated with candles and pastry. This artificial, candle-covered tree, together with a flat triangle-shaped candle rack called a *lichstock*, played an important role in the eventual development of the candle-lit Christmas tree, but for a long time it was common practice for a room to contain both a candle-lit pyramid or *lichstock* and a candleless *Christbaum*. Pyramid and *Christbaum* existed side by side for many generations before the first candles were transferred to the branches of the tree.

Trees in the eighteenth century were decorated with many kinds of sweet confections, as well as gold-leaf-covered apples and other gilded fruits and nuts. In 1755 it was recorded that Berliners even gilded potatoes, but the emphasis was primarily on edible ornaments—decorative candies and cookies—so much so that in some areas the tree was called a "sugartree."

Johann Wolfgang von Goethe set up such a tree in 1769 for the children of a friend in Leipzig. In his novel *The Sorrows of Young*

A Christmas tree in Queen Victoria's sitting room at Windsor. The uniquely shaped tree is a *tanne*, brought from the German forest that surrounded Albert's boyhood home in Coburg.

Werther, he had his heroine, Lotte, describe a sugartree with fruits and sweetmeats and lighted candles.

In 1798 Samuel Taylor Coleridge spent Christmas in a German home, and wrote back to England about the tree:

On the evening before Christmas Day, one of the parlors is lighted up by the children, into which the parents must not go; a great yew bough is fastened on the table at a distance from the wall, a multitude of little tapers are fixed to the bough, but not so as to burn it till they are nearly consumed, and coloured paper, etc., hangs and flutters from the twigs. Under this bough the children lay out in great order the presents they mean to give their parents, still concealing in their pockets what they intend to give each other. Then the parents are introduced, and each presents his little gift; they then bring out the remainder one by one, from their pockets and present them with kisses and embraces. I was very much affected. The shadow of the bough and its appendages on the wall and arching over the ceiling made a pretty picture.

In most cases, to the tremendous delight of the children and adults alike, sugartrees were shaken and the sweets eaten. This usually took place on the evening of January 6, known as Twelfth Night, or Epiphany, the feast commemorating the arrival of the Magi at Bethlehem.

Although Christmas trees first captured the fancy of the patrician class, it was not long before well-to-do merchants in northern German cities and towns took up the practice. Peasants, however, were slow to adopt trees compared to their more fashionable city brethren. And Catholics were slower than Lutherans, who identified the tree with Martin Luther.

In Catholic Bavaria the focal point of the Christmas celebration for centuries had been the "crib," a manger scene lovingly decorated. In the 1860s if the pious Bavarian had a "tree," it was a Christmas pyramid, its bare shelves bearing only cards cut in the shape of bells, stars, and crosses and imprinted with Biblical texts and religious poems.

In the mid-nineteenth century the tree's spread in Lutheran northern Germany was phenomenal, thanks to a legend and some popular reproductions of a particular painting of Martin Luther. In 1845, almost three hundred years after Luther's death, an artist named C. A. Schwerdgeburth painted Luther and his family seated around a shining, candle-covered Christmas tree in 1536. According to an old story, Luther was out walking on Christmas Eve, when the stars gave him the idea of putting numerous candles on a fir tree to impress his son with the message of Christmas—that the Christ Child was the light of the world. Today historians call this mere folklore, since the first evidence of a lighted tree of any sort appears more than a century after Luther's death in 1546.

Another popular Christmas tree myth that should be identified as such concerns Prince Albert, Queen Victoria's husband. Albert came from the German province of Saxe-Coburg and is generally credited with introducing the Christmas tree to England after the birth of their first son in 1841. In reality, however, he simply popularized a custom known to members of the English royal family for at least half a century. Dr. John Watkins, a member of the court of Queen Charlotte, Victoria's grandmother and wife of George III, once recalled for historians the presence of a Christmas tree in the Queen's Lodge at Windsor on Christmas Day in 1800. "In the middle of the room stood an immense tub with a yew tree placed in it, from the branches of which hung bunches of sweetmeats, almonds, and raisins in papers, fruits, and toys, most tastefully arranged, and the whole illuminated by small wax candles." We also know that one of Victoria's aunts, Queen Adelaide, the wife of England's King William IV, always had a tree for her Christmas Eve parties in the Dragon Room at Brighton Pavilion. And on December 24, 1832, thirteen-year-old Victoria wrote in her diary: "After dinner we went upstairs. We went into the drawing room near the dining room. There were two large round tables on which were placed the trees hung with lights and sugar ornaments. All the presents being placed around the trees." Possibly the origin of the story about Prince Albert's connection with Christmas trees was a full-page illustration in an 1848 edition of the *Illustrated London News* showing one of Albert's trees at Windsor. The picture captured the imagination of the English middle class, and the custom spread rapidly, since Victorians were given to imitating the royal family. To give Albert his due, however, he did more than merely provide an example, for each Christmas he presented decorated trees to schools and army barracks.

Albert's personal candle-lit trees seem to have been decorated almost entirely with sweets of the most expensive kind. From the branches hung elegant tiny trays, baskets, bonbonnières, and other

An American engraver copied the English version of Victoria and her family for *Godey's Lady's Book* in 1850, altering a few details, including the ornaments.

BELOW: A nineteenth-century woodcut of a Christmas tree with ornaments.

The famous English engraving of Victoria and Albert, their children, and their tree at Windsor Castle in 1848.

receptacles for candy, glacé fruits, and gilt-covered gingerbread prepared largely in the royal household's kitchens. On top stood the small figure of an angel with outstretched wings, holding a wreath in each hand.

Although Victoria kept and treasured all of Albert's possessions until her own death in 1901, this figure and all of his other tree ornaments have since disappeared without trace. In the royal archives is a photograph of one of Albert's trees taken at Windsor in 1860. A later photograph shows that Victoria had adopted the German court's custom of giving an individually decorated tree to each of her children.

Outside of court circles, the Christmas tree made its first appearance in England as early as 1822 in the homes of German merchants residing in Manchester. In 1850 Charles Dickens gave his readers a vivid description of the new fashion in a magazine article:

I have been looking on, this evening, at a merry company of children assembled round that pretty German toy, a Christmas tree. The tree was planted in the middle of a great round table, and towered high above their heads. It was brilliantly lighted by a multitude of little tapers; and everywhere sparkled and glittered with bright objects. There were rosy-cheeked dolls, hiding behind green leaves; and there were real watches (with movable hands, at least, and an endless capacity of being wound up) dangling from innumerable twigs; there were French polished tables, chairs, bedsteads, wardrobes, eight-day clocks, and various other articles of domestic furniture (wonderfully made in tin) perched among the boughs, as if in preparation for some fairy housekeeping; there were jolly, broad-faced little men, much more agreeable in appearance than many real men—and no wonder, for their heads took off, and showed them to be full of sugarplums; there were fiddles and drums; there were tambourines, books, work boxes, paint boxes; there were trinkets for the elder girls, far brighter than any grown-up gold and jewels; there were baskets and pin cushions in all devices; there were guns, swords and banners; there were witches standing in enchanted rings of pasteboard, to tell fortunes; there were teetotums [a child's toy similar to a top but spun by the fingers instead of string], humming tops, needle cases, pen wipers, smelling bottles, conversation cards, bouquet holders, real fruit, made artificially dazzling with gold leaf; imitation apples, pears, walnuts, crammed with surprises; in short, as a pretty child before me de-

22

lightedly whispered to another pretty child, her bosom friend, "There was everything, and more." This motley collection of odd objects, clustering on the tree like magic fruit, and flashing back the bright looks directed towards it from every side—some of the diamond eyes admiring it were hardly on a level with the table, and a few were languishing in timid wonder on the bosoms of pretty mothers, aunts, and nurses—made lively realisation of the fancies of childhood; and set me thinking how all the trees that grow and all the things that come into existence on the earth, have their wild adornments at that well remembered time.

This is the only account of "the new German toy" that Dickens, the great author of Christmas tales, ever wrote. Though his name is synonymous with our ideas of how to keep Christmas, there is no mention of a Christmas tree in *A Christmas Carol,* written in 1843, or in any of his later Christmas novels and short stories.

The Christmas tree never became a universal custom in England, as it would become in Germany and America, probably because of the lack of an inexpensive and ready supply of evergreens.

On both sides of the Atlantic Christmas trees were popularized around the turn of the twentieth century by annual accounts in news-papers and magazines of the German royal family's Christmas trees. As the Kaiser's family grew, so did the number of his royal trees. Each year he set up on tables and decorated numerous trees in varying sizes, according to the size of the recipient. In 1906, at his palace in Potsdam, he had a record twelve trees, one each for himself, his wife, six sons, three daughters, and one grandchild.

Germany thus gave the world a beautifully and imaginatively decorated table-size tree, but it was in America that the Christmas tree would grow up to reach from floor to ceiling.

II
THE CHRISTMAS TREE
GROWS UP IN AMERICA

T he first Christmas trees we know of in America were those decorated for the children in the German Moravian church's communal settlement at Bethlehem, Pennsylvania, on Christmas Day in 1747. These were not real evergreens, but the European style of wooden pyramids covered with evergreen boughs. A diary tells us that "for this occasion several small pyramids and one large pyramid of green brushwood had been prepared, all decorated with candles and the large one with apples and pretty verses."

There is a popular story which says that the Hessian soldiers surprised by Washington and his troops at Trenton on Christmas night, 1776, had been celebrating around a candle-lit Christmas tree. Today historians can find no documentary evidence for this story in diaries or letters left by either the German mercenaries or Americans who were present at the battle. Despite this, there is the possibility that there was a Christmas tree in Trenton that night, since we know that there were some trees in the Hessians' homeland at that period.

Christmas in an American home c. 1895.

This previously unpublished sketch by the
Philadelphia artist John Lewis Krimmel is
one of two Christmas drawings from his
sketchbooks of 1819 and 1820.

Before the 1850s references to Christmas trees in America were extremely spotty. The second oldest record occurs almost three-quarters of a century after the first, in the form of two sketchbook drawings by John Lewis Krimmel, a Philadelphia artist who made them in 1819 or 1820.

On December 20, 1821, Matthew Zahm wrote in his diary: "Sally and our Thomas and William Hensel was out for Christmas trees on the hill at Kendrich's saw mill." Zahm and his family lived seventy miles southwest of Bethlehem in Lancaster County.

Two years later, on December 23, 1823, across the broad Susquehanna River in York County, an interesting item appeared in the *York Gazette*. It reported, in the quaint Pennsylvania-German dialect of the time, that the society of bachelors was accepting a cartload of ginger cakes from its counterpart, the old maids' society, in return for which the bachelors had decided to set up a decorated "Kris Kringle Tree."

The oldest record we have of Christmas trees in a major American city was in 1825, when Philadelphia's *Saturday Evening Post* described "trees visible through the windows, whose green boughs are laden with fruit, richer than the golden apples of the Hesperides, or the sparkling diamonds that clustered on the branches in the wonderful cave of Aladdin."

It was in Massachusetts, however, rather than Pennsylvania that the most widely read early account of a Christmas tree was published. In a penny pamphlet distributed by the American Sunday School Union of Boston, Harriet Martineau, unaware of the Pennsylvania trees, mistakenly gave credit for the first Christmas tree in America to Charles Follen, a German living in Boston. She described his 1832 tree:

I was present at the introduction into the new country of the spectacle of the German Christmas tree. My little friend Charley [Follen's son] and three companions had been long preparing for this pretty show. The cook had broken eggs carefully in the middle for some weeks past, that Charley might have the shells for cups; and these cups were gilded and coloured very prettily. We were all engaged in sticking on the last seven dozen of wax tapers, and in filling the gilded egg-cups and gay paper cornucopiae with comfits, lozenges, barley sugar. The tree was the top of a young fir, planted in a tub, which was ornamented with moss. Smart dolls and other whimsies glittered in the evergreen, and there was not a twig which had not something sparkling upon it.

It really looked beautiful; the room seemed in a blaze, and the ornaments were so well hung on that no accident happened, except that one doll's petticoat caught fire. There was a sponge tied to the end of a stick to put out any supernumerary blaze, and no harm ensued. I mounted the steps behind the tree to see the effect of opening the doors. It was delightful. The children poured in, but in a moment every voice was hushed. Their faces were upturned to the blaze, all eyes wide open, all lips parted, all steps arrested. Nobody spoke, only Charley leaped for joy. The first symptom of recovery was the children's wandering around the tree. At last, a quick pair of eyes discovered that it bore something eatable, and from that moment the babble began again. . . . I have little doubt the Christmas tree will become one of the most flourishing exotics of New England.

In 1833 Constantin Hering, a young doctor from Leipzig, arrived in Philadelphia. During his first December in America, homesickness and the memories of his boyhood led him to cross the Delaware River with a friend to cut Christmas trees. Back in Philadelphia with trees on their shoulders, they were followed by a band of curious children. Each year for the next half century, Dr. Hering's marvelous creation was displayed publicly on certain evenings for his friends and for his patients and their friends who wanted to see a German Christmas tree.

On that same Christmas of 1833 Gustave Koerner, a German settler, was living in St. Clair County, Illinois. Since that countryside on the banks of the Mississippi was without evergreens, Koerner and his friends erected their own makeshift Christmas tree. They decorated a sassafras tree with candles, apples, sweets, ribbons, bright paper, hazelnuts and hickory nuts, and polished red haws, the fruit of the hawthorn tree.

Because the novelty of Christmas trees seldom failed to draw a crowd, clever fundraisers came up with the idea of displaying them in order to raise money for charities. The first such tree was advertised in 1830 by the Dorcas Society of York, an association of ladies that

clothed poor widows and orphans. The enterprising ladies collected six and a half cents each for tickets to see a decorated tree at the society's annual holiday fair.

With people paying to see Christmas trees, it was only a matter of time until a born entrepreneur had the same idea. In 1840 the following advertisement appeared three times in the York *Pennsylvania Republican*:

Christmas Tree. For the amusement of the ladies and Gentlemen of York, and its vicinity, GOODRIDGE, will exhibit at his residence, in East Philadelphia Street, a CHRISTMAS TREE, the exhibition of which will commence on Christmas Eve, and continue, Sunday excepted, until New Year. Tickets to be had at his store.

The earliest Christmas tree in American literature appeared in the *Token and Atlantic Souvenir* in 1836. In the story a German maid was persuaded by her mistress to decorate a tree with gifts after the custom of her homeland. The author, Miss Sedwick, gave her readers the following description of the tree which the mistress and maid decorated after secretly carrying it to the library:

The sturdiest branch drooped with its burden of books, chess men, puzzles, etc. for Julius, a strippling of 13, dolls, birds, beasts, and boxes were hung on the lesser limbs. A regiment of soldiers had alighted on one bough, and Noah's ark was anchored to another, and to all the slender branches were attached cherries, plumbs, strawberries and fine peaches, as tempting and at least as sweet as the fruits of paradise.

The first Christmas tree in Williamsburg, Virginia, appeared in 1842. Charles Minnigerode, a young, German-born teacher at the College of William and Mary, decorated a small evergreen tree to amuse the children of his friend Professor Nathaniel Beverly Tucker. Minnigerode wired candles to its branches and decorated it with popcorn, nuts, colored-paper decorations, and a gold star.

As German settlers continued to push into the American West, they took their Christmas custom with them. In 1846 a traveler's

31

An 1870 Christmas tree decorated almost entirely with candles and toys.

letter told of a Christmas tree decorated by German farmers homesteading in Texas. There is no record of when the first evergreen was decorated on the West Coast, but in 1862 a naturalist, William Brewer, visited San Francisco and wrote that he found "Christmas trees are the custom."

Not every German family in America had a Christmas tree, particularly during the first half of the nineteenth century. The custom was still spreading in Germany at that time, and it would not become universal, even there, until the end of the century. Nevertheless, German immigrants were responsible for bringing the Christmas tree to America.

In the mid-nineteenth century Dutch families in New York adopted candlelit trees, but they decorated them for the New Year rather than Christmas. Santa Claus also arrived a week late, carrying New Year's rather than Christmas presents.

Magazines and newspapers played an important role in popularizing the custom among Americans of other backgrounds. Printed references to Christmas trees were scarce at first and were not always entirely favorable. Although the Christmas tree would seem to have been an irresistible idea, it was in fact attacked by many critics for its pagan origins. Even as late as 1878 a New York reporter described the custom, no longer entirely unique to the German population, as "an aboriginal oddity."

In 1883 a *New York Times* editor criticized the "German Christmas tree," calling it "a rootless and lifeless corpse—never worthy of the day." Ironically, he predicted that the Christmas tree had had its day and was being replaced by a return to the Christmas stocking of his own childhood. The stocking-versus-tree debate continued for many Christmases. Happily for later generations, the conflict was eventually resolved by a majority of American parents, who simply adopted both child-pleasing customs.

The Christmas tree made its first appearance in an American women's magazine in 1850 when *Godey's Lady's Book* adapted the famous picture of Queen Victoria and her family's tree printed by the *Illustrated London News* two years earlier. The *Godey's* engraver borrowed heavily from his English source, copying Albert's German tree exactly, but Americanizing the family by removing Victoria's crown and a few other royal details. Close examination of the two engravings reveals that the engraver also changed a great many of the ornaments.

Despite this appearance in *Godey's Lady's Book* and occasional references in other publications such as *Harper's Weekly, Gleason's Pictorial Drawing Room Companion,* and *Scribner's Magazine,* the spread of the new custom was slow and not always smooth.

The first Christmas tree to appear in an American church caused a real furor. In 1851 the Reverend Henry Schwan, a 32-year-old German immigrant who had arrived in America less than a year before, placed a Christmas tree in his church in Cleveland, Ohio. Some members of his congregation immediately branded it a throwback to pagan customs. Upset by this resistance to a Christmas decoration traditional in the churches of his native Hanover, Reverend Schwan decided to have no tree the following year. On Christmas Eve, however, another Cleveland minister, Edwin Canfield, settled the matter in favor of the Christmas tree by having two children deliver a tree to Pastor Schwan and his congregation.

In 1853 and again in 1855 Sarah Hale, the *Godey's* fashion-setting editor, mentioned the custom of Christmas trees. In her December 1860 issue she published a story by Lizzie McIntyre portraying the Christmas Eve of a widowed doctor and his daughters. The story gave a detailed description of a typical tree of that period when candles, food, ribbon, homemade paper decorations, and small toys were the only ornaments available:

The square of green baize being tacked down, a large stone jar was placed in the middle of it, and in this the tree stood nobly erect. Damp sand was put around the stem till the large green tree stood firmly in place. A flounce of green chintz round the jar concealed its stony ugliness, and over the top, round the tree, was a soft cushion of moss. It was a large evergreen, reaching almost to the ceiling, for all the family presents were to be placed upon it. This finished, the process of dressing commenced. From a basket in the corner, Marion drew long strings of bright red holly berries, threaded like beads upon fine cord. These were festooned in graceful garlands from the boughs of the tree. While Marion was thus employed, Grace and the Doctor arranged the tiny tapers. This was a delicate task. Long pieces of fine wire were passed through the taper at the bottom, and these clasped over the stem of each branch, and twisted together underneath. Great care was taken that there should be clear space above each wick, that nothing might catch fire.

Strings of bright berries, small bouquets of paper flowers, strings of beads, tiny flags of gay ribbons, stars and shields of gilt paper, lace bags filled with colored candies, knots of bright ribbons, all homemade by Marion's and Grace's skillful fingers, made a brilliant show at a trifling cost, the basket seeming possessed of unheard-of capacities, to judge from the multitude and variety of articles the sisters drew from it.

Meantime, upon the wick of each little taper the Doctor rubbed with his finger a drop of alcohol to insure its lighting quickly. This was a process he trusted to no one else, for fear the spirit might fall upon some part of the tree not meant to catch fire. At last, all the contents of the basket were on the tree and then the more important presents were brought down from an upper room. There were many articles seemingly too clumsy for the tree, but Marion passed around them gay colored ribbons, till they formed a basket work and looped them over the branches till even Hester's workbox looked graceful. Dolls for each of the little girls were seated on the boughs, and a large cart for Eddie, with two horses prancing before it, drove gaily amongst the top branches, as if each steed possessed the wings of Pegasus. On the moss beneath the branches, Marion placed a set of wooden animals for Eddie, while from the top-most branch was suspended a gilded cage ready for the canary bird Dr. Gratley had purchased for the pet-loving Lizzie.

Various mysterious packages wrapped in paper and marked Grace, Marion, or Papa were put aside that all the delicious mystery of Christmas might be preserved. At length, all was ready, and, carefully locking the doors, the trio went up to their respective rooms.

This 1860 reference is of particular value because it describes a large tree that stood on the floor instead of on a table, like its smaller German predecessors. Indeed, the idea of a great floor-to-ceiling Christmas tree is uniquely American. The account also reflected a custom that flourished in America in the last century, one that all but disappeared in the early years of this one—the placing of gifts on the tree itself. In 1901 it was reported that, while spruces were better-looking Christmas trees, balsam firs were generally preferred because their

A Christmas stocking, manufactured c. 1895. At this time, most stockings were those actually worn by the children who hung them, unlike this commercially produced example.

A Christmas tree, 1882.

branches did not grow quite so close together and thus gave more room for the presents upon them.

Most early trees were less elaborately and expensively decorated than the one in the *Godey's* story. Many were decorated entirely with simple things like cookies, candy, pine cones, dried seed pods, and strings of popcorn and cranberries. A small yellow apple with shiny red cheeks called a "ladies apple" was a popular tree decoration, and some Pennsylvania Dutch farmers' trees were decorated only with home-made doughnuts and strings of dried apple slices. Throughout the nineteenth century German-Americans had a great fondness for paper flowers, paper mottoes, and white sugar animals, often as brightly and imaginatively painted as pieces of Mexican folk art.

The arrival in America of German-made glass balls brought about a major change in the way the American tree was decorated, by introducing the universal Christmas ornament of the twentieth century and triggering the revolutionary shift from homemade to store-bought decorations.

The first glass ornaments, which were glass icicles and heavy glass balls, probably reached America around 1860, transported along with the treasured household possessions of unknown families of German immigrants. For another twenty years glass ornaments were rare in American parlors, although their first commercial importation began as early as 1870. One year later a New York glassmaker, William DeMuth, produced and advertised the first American-made "silvered" glass balls and chains of beads for Christmas trees.

At first glass ornaments were sold on street corners in German communities, but by the early 1880s a few toy and variety stores were selling Christmas tree "dressings." A decade later the number and the diversity of the ornaments had become awesome.

Chains of balls began to appear in the 1870s. "We hung on our Christmas tree strands of large round glass beads that shine like mirrors and are very light in weight. Uncle brought these ornaments from Paris, a novelty . . . ," wrote one Sophie Palmette in her diary in 1876.

In 1883 Erlich Brothers, a New York toy wholesaler, published a catalogue listing fancy glass balls in various bright colors. These were said to add greatly to the effect of a Christmas tree, reflecting and softening the light of the hanging candles. The Erlichs also advertised three types of candleholders, a large variety of silver and gold paper ornaments, and small transparent gelatin lanterns and banners for the tree.

Ten years later Amos M. Lyon, another New York toy importer, included three full pages of Christmas tree ornaments in his toy-and-doll catalogue. He offered four sizes of wax angels with spun-glass wings; glass tree ornaments "in all conceivable shapes" including round, oblong, heart, balloon, acorn, bird, fruit and so on; three sizes of glass tree points for the top of the tree; tinsel ornaments in a wide array of shapes and colors. He also showed silver and gilt paper and cardboard ornaments in many shapes including stars, leaves, comets, drums, slippers, animals, and fish. And he had gelatin candy ornaments such as tiny vases, trumpets, cannons, and acorns; and also miniature pieces of kitchen equipment—bottles and rolling pins, and even an inch-high potato masher.

Lyon's catalogue also listed fancy versions of the extremely popular homemade cornucopias, those cone-shaped holders for nuts, candy, and crystallized fruit that we invariably envision on Christmas trees of the 1890s. He also had a profusion of sizes and shapes of tiny silk and puffed-satin candy boxes.

Wholesalers like Lyon and the Erlichs also supplied America with great quantities of white cotton batting for Christmas tree snow. The December issues of 1890s magazines such as the *Ladies' Home Journal* advocated laying pieces of cotton along the limbs to simulate snow. It was easy, inexpensive, and the effect was pleasing. Cotton batting was originally produced for use in quilts, but a lot of it was used for old-time Christmas trees, either on them or spread out on the floor to cover a makeshift tree holder and provide a snowy setting for the tree. Aside from its aesthetic contribution, it also protected the floor from dripping candle wax.

Many antique ornaments still have wax drippings left by one or more candles that were attached somewhere above them on a tree. It wasn't until 1917 that the Standard Oil Company of New York, under its trade name Socony, put out an improved Christmas tree candle it advertised as "dripless."

The romantic idea of a snow-covered Christmas tree led to several unusual subcategories. Thrifty German farmers in Pennsylvania stripped Christmas trees of their needles after they were dried out and placed

37

the skeleton in the attic. The following year the tree was brought down again and wrapped in cotton, so that it resembled a tree in the forest after a snow storm, and then it was decorated. After Christmas the tree was returned to the attic, where it was covered with old newspapers to keep the cotton clean.

A similar custom developed in which winter barren trees were cut, brought in, and wrapped with cotton snow. A good tree for this purpose was the sassafras, which in parts of the eastern United States grew like a weed along the divisions between farmers' fields. Farmers considered sassafras nearly worthless trees and were usually glad to give them away. Early in the twentieth century, when the natural supply of evergreens began to be decimated by the increasingly popular Christmas tree custom, the editors of many magazines showed their readers how to make this artificial snow-covered Christmas tree and recommended its use.

As wonderful as the old-fashioned, store-bought trimmings were, proof that they were not essential was supplied by a newspaper's 1898 description of Christmas trees on the farms around Reading, Pennsylvania:

> Tinsel, spangles and colored glass have but little place on the country Christmas tree. Instead there are huge honey cakes, ginger cakes cut into shapes representing great fat hogs, sheep, rabbits, cats, horses, cows and other farm animal life. Some of these animal cakes are several feet square and made attractive by sprinkling of red, white and blue sugars.
> Perched on branches of the tree are stuffed squirrels, chipmunks, and other trophies of the hunt and the country boy's skill with the shotgun, while grouped around the base of the tree are opossums, raccoons, and, occasionally, Christmas greens and brilliant-hued ribbons. The tree is also laden with chunks of home-made taffy, large red apples and winter pears, with a sprinkling of shell barks, chestnuts, and other productions of the farm.

Photographs taken around the turn of the century show that the average American Christmas tree often had relatively few store-bought ornaments. Most families added to their collection one a Christmas—big ornaments in prosperous years and small ones, if any at all, in poor

A photograph made in 1893 in western New York State of a doctor's son and his tree, which was sparsely decorated, with only six glass ornaments.

years. The rest of the trimmings were still homemade and the December issues of women's magazines began to feature do-it-yourself directions for making them, just as they do today.

Only one American family in five had a Christmas tree in 1900, although most children probably enjoyed one at their school or at a neighbor's house and undoubtedly wished for one of their own. In the first years of the twentieth century the custom spread like wildfire, and by 1910 in many parts of America, nearly all children had a tree at home. Nevertheless, there were many little towns in the South and in the West where the first tree did not appear until after 1915, and in some areas it was customary to have a church or community-hall tree but rare to see one in the home. There are a surprising number of Americans alive today who never saw a Christmas tree as children and never had their own until they became adults.

By 1930 the tree had become a nearly universal part of the American Christmas. Throughout the Depression, a generation of Americans dug deep into their pockets to give their families a tree like the ones they had loved or desperately wanted as children. Today the big tree in the living room, the little one on the office desk, and the artificial tree without which it wouldn't be Christmas at the roadside hamburger palace all bespeak a deep national love of America's adopted Christmas custom.

OPPOSITE: A page of Christmas tree ornaments from Ehrich's Fashion Quarterly, Winter 1882.

This 1893 engraving reminds us that Santa Claus used to bring children their Christmas trees along with their toys.

OVERLEAF: Christmas morning in 1867. This engraving from *Harper's Weekly* seems to show glass ornaments, which would have been extremely rare in America at the time.

CHRISTMAS-TREE ORNAMENTS, ETC.

CHRISTMAS-TREE CANDLES, Etc.

1. Christmas-Tree Candles, assorted colors. These candles come packed in pound boxes, containing either 24, 36, 48, or 72 candles. By the pound only. Price, per pound.................$0 35

(By mail, 20c extra.)

No. 2.

No. 3.

No. 4.

2. Plain Brackets to hold candles. Per doz.   04
3. With **Swinging Ball Balance.** Per doz.   21

(By mail, 6c and 18c extra.)

4. Combination Candle and Bracket Cones. Will burn for three hours without dripping, or danger of fire. Price, per doz........... 45

(By mail, 15c extra.)

5. Fancy Glass Balls, in various bright colors. These balls add greatly to the effect of a Christmas-Tree, the bright colored balls reflecting and softening the light of the hanging candles. Put up in boxes of 25 to 100 each. Price, per box, 20c, 30c, 40c, 50c, and...................... 75

6. Fancy Silver and Gilt Ornaments, representing hearts, shields, globes, crosses, fishes, etc. Each ornament is formed of two pieces of embossed silver or gilt stiffened paper, firmly fixed together, so that it presents exactly the same appearance on either side. Price, per doz...........$0 10

(By mail, 5c extra.)

7. Same style, larger and finer. Price, per doz.   25

(By mail, 5c extra.)

8. Embossed Gold and Silver Fish, seven inches long. Price, each, 5c; per doz........... 50

(By mail, 8c extra.)

9. Embossed Gold and Silver Dogs, four inches long. Price, each, 5c; per doz........... 50

(By mail, 8c extra.)

10. Embossed Gold and Silver Clocks, four and one half inches high. Price, each, 5c; per doz....................................... 50

(By mail, 8c extra.)

11. Embossed Gold and Silver Trumpets, large size. Price, each, 5c; per doz.............. 50

(By mail, 10c extra.)

12. Embossed Gold and Silver Crosses, five and one half inches long. Price, each, 5c; per doz....................................... 50

(By mail, 8c extra.)

13. Dressed Paper Dolls, six inches long. Price, each, 5c; per doz....................... 50

(By mail, 10c extra.)

14. Gelatine and Gold Drums. Price, each, 5c; per doz...................................$0 50

(By mail, 8c extra.)

15. Assortments of the Ornaments described above, containing some of each kind. By the dozen only. Price, per doz...................... 50

16. Fancy Straw and Gilt Ornaments, assorted. Price, each, 5c; per doz.............. 50

(By mail, 8c extra.)

17. Larger and Finer Ornaments, in embossed gilt and silver paper, and gelatine; embracing stars, shells, gondolas, slippers, tea-pots, lamps, boots, angels, lanterns, beetles, etc. Price, each, 10c; per doz., assorted.................... 1 00

(By mail, 10c extra.)

18. Transparent Gelatine Lanterns. Price, each, 6c; per doz................................ 60

(By mail, 8c extra.)

19. Very Fine Embossed Gold Angels, six and one half inches long. Price, each, 8c; per doz... 80

(By mail, 10c extra.)

20. Same, eight inches long. Price, each, 12c; per doz....................... .... 1 20

(By mail, 12c extra.)

21. Gelatine Banners, with appropriate mottoes in gold. Price, each, 5c; per doz............ 50

(By mail, 8c extra.)

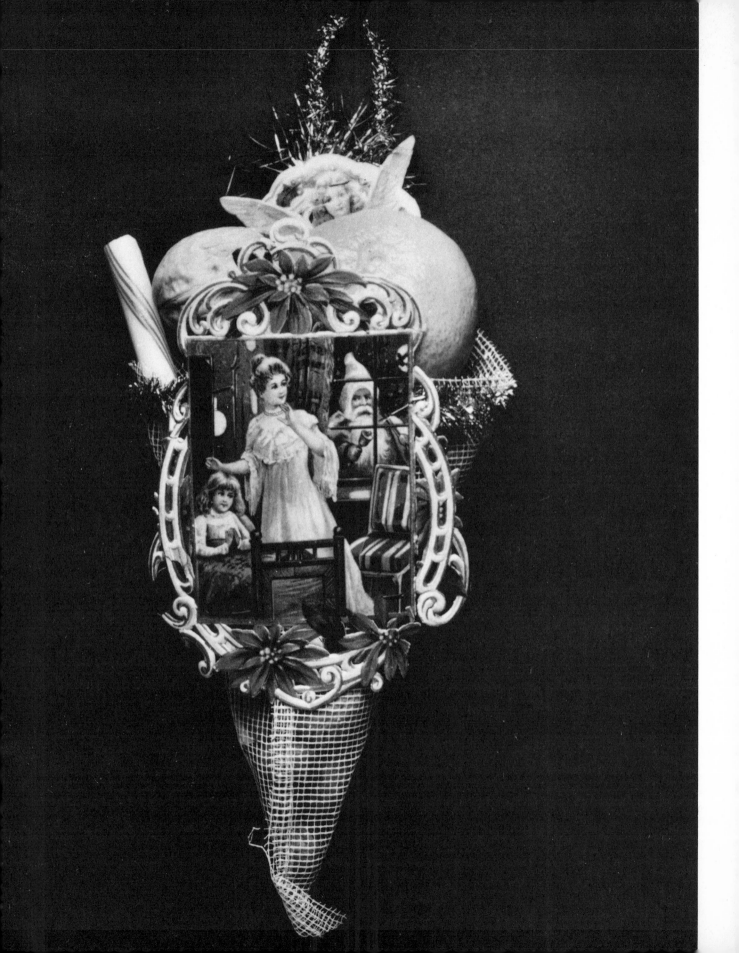

III
COOKIES, NUTS,
AND SUGAR PLUMS

mong the Germans in Pennsylvania, America's earliest Christmas trees, like their European predecessors, almost always included cookies in their homemade decorations. Even before there were Christmas trees in America, most housewives had a fancy cookie mold or a few cookie cutters that came out only at Christmas.

Sweet cookies have always been an important part of the Christmas festivities of northern Europe, and to the Germans from the area in which the Christmas tree originated, the decorative baking of figurative cookies is an age-old art.

From the beginning of the nineteenth century, the Pennsylvania Germans decorated their trees with *matzebaum*, wafer-thin, two-by-four-inch cakes made from almond paste, sugar, and egg whites. Before being baked, each cake was pressed with a carved wooden mold that left raised images of animals, birds, or flowers on the face of the cookie. Most of them were eaten by the children when the Christmas tree was dismantled, but a few were laid away and brought out to decorate the family tree year after year. If *matzebaum* were being

45

A net cornucopia. Note the old-fashioned Santa Claus looking through the window.

made purely for decoration, thrifty cooks seldom used almond paste, but rather corn meal or wheat flour and glue to save money. One old cookie with a rooster striding across it was baked and dated as long ago as 1823. It was originally used on a tree set up each Christmas in the "long room" of the Lamb Tavern, a Lancaster, Pennsylvania, hostelry. After slow baking at a low temperature, *matzebaum* were usually painted with homemade vegetable dyes and many of them were dated.

Thicker silhouette shapes were pressed from the same type of almond-flavored dough and called marzipan or marchpane. Because of the soft consistency of the dough, round shapes were preferred, such as lifelike miniature fruits and vegetables. Marzipan originated in Persia and had been made in Germany since the Middle Ages. It was originally a delicacy consumed at court banquets and became a common Christmas confection during the latter part of the eighteenth century.

Another cookie commonly hung on the Christmas tree was the white *springerle,* made of an egg dough seasoned with anise seeds. The smoothly rising dough produced an excellent cameolike image when molded, and the motif-bearing cookies, which were occasionally painted, like *matzebaum* and marzipan, were then hung from the tree with a piece of string or a ribbon. Most of the old *springerle* molds are so skillfully carved from soft, fine-grained woods such as pear and boxwood that we know they were the work of professional German woodcarvers. Although some old molds were probably carved in America, the majority were undoubtedly brought to this country by the flood of German immigrants that settled here throughout the eighteenth and nineteenth centuries.

Housewives of German-Swiss descent made *tirggel,* a similar but thinner molded cookie made from honey, flour, sugar, and water. In the oven the pictorial relief turned slightly browner than the rest of the cookie, which was translucent when held against the light of a Christmas tree candle.

While comparatively few families possessed these specialized kinds of cookie molds, most households had cookie cutters, often made by itinerant tinsmiths. With them a German housewife cut out such Christmas favorites as butter cracknels—flat, hard, brittle, sugar-and-flour-based cookies made in the shape of moons, stars, hearts, trees, tulips, and *distelfink*—the goldfinches so often drawn by Pennsylvania artists. Every woman liked to have at least one shape that nobody else had, and so an infinite variety of designs existed, including eventually the new American character Uncle Sam. Many of these handmade tin cookie cutters had shallow inset pieces for the addition of details like an eye for the cat or a wing for the bird.

Most of the cookies on nineteenth-century Christmas trees were thicker than today's cookies: Spice, butter, and gingerbread cookies were often half an inch thick. White cookies were frequently sprinkled with red sugar, "for pretty," as the Pennsylvania Dutch still say. Cookie-baking binges often lasted for two solid weeks early in December. A "washbasketful" was a standard of measure for cookies in Pennsylvania-Dutch kitchens. The housewife who didn't have at least several washbaskets full of cookies just wasn't ready for Christmas.

The counterpart of the usual thick cookie was the rich sandtart. It was a matter of pride among the women to roll their sandtart dough thinner than anybody else's. The name comes from a top glazing of mixed raw egg white and yolk, over which sugar and cinnamon were sprinkled. Traditionally, each paper-thin sandtart was decorated with half a hickory nut.

By the 1880s, in addition to gingerbread animals and the now-classic gingerbread man, flat gingerbread cakes were hung on the trees. Instead of raised decorations, never entirely successful with soft-textured gingerbread dough, they were decorated with colorful pictures pasted on with egg white. By this time shiny, embossed chromolithographic pictures, like those in Victorian scrapbooks, were much in vogue. There were Christmas motifs—the Holy Family, angels, children carrying fir trees, and Santa Claus—and poetic images such as entwined hands, babies in cradles, billing and cooing doves, and little churches.

Pretzel-shaped cookies, as well as actual pretzels, were familiar ornaments on numerous German-American *Christbaums*. To the devout, the shape of the twisted ring represented hands in the attitude of prayer.

One type of cookie, the tragant, was made almost exclusively for ornaments. Although tragants looked good enough to eat, they were not very appetizing after the first bite. The dough was fine grained, hard, durable, and could easily be painted or iced. It was made with a gum

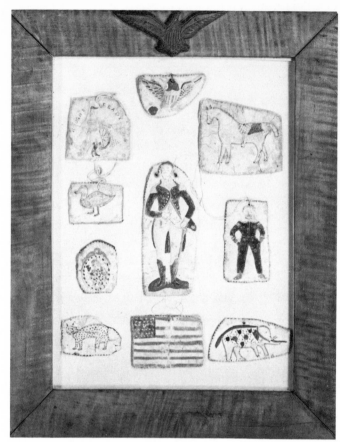

Old marzipan cookie ornaments, from the
collection of the Winterthur Museum in
Delaware.

A modern *springerle* cookie, made in an
old wooden mold.

called tragacanth, which served as the binding agent for the sugar and starch and gave the cookie its name. The dough was ideal for free-hand molding, and baskets of flowers, birds, trumpets, and Christ Child dolls were fashioned from it. These were dried in a warm oven, then colorfully glazed with bright sugar icings. Intricate three-dimensional trim was often added with a miniature pastry tube.

To this country's German-Americans, *apfel, nuss, und mandelkern* (apples, nuts, and almonds) were the traditional foods of Christmas, and all three were hung on their Christmas trees in various sizes and shapes. Apples were usually hung by their stems, but slices of dried apple were often strung into chains that predated the characteristic American innovations of popcorn and cranberries. *Schnitz* is the Pennsylvania-Dutch word for dried pieces of apple. The slices, or quarters, could be peeled, although in the case of sweet apples they were usually left unpared. So that they would not turn brown, the *schnitz* were "cured" with sulfur. In 1857 a German-language news-paper in Tiffin, Ohio, even described a tree decorated in the old German manner with gilded apples. Nuts were hung on the tree in many ways—gilded with gold leaf or wrapped in tin foil, dipped in flour, or painted with bright colors.

Popcorn, the ingredient of innumerable homemade decorations, was used in several ways. As early as the 1860s there were references to it being strung and hung drooping from the branches of home and Sunday-school trees. Hanging balls of caramelized popcorn were endlessly popular suggestions in ladies' magazines around the turn of the century.

By 1900, at the suggestion of the same magazines, people were dyeing their popcorn with food coloring to produce red or green chains. Strings of mixed red, white, and green popcorn were very attractive against the dark green branches from which they were draped in enormous loops. For variety, women were encouraged to intersperse red cranberries between the white pieces of popcorn.

For most families, shelling, popping, and stringing popcorn was a time-consuming but extremely pleasant way to pass a pre-Christmas evening or two. Affluent city people who were too busy to make their own could often purchase ready-made popcorn strings from street vendors whose own wives and children were their primary source of supply.

OPPOSITE: Homemade
paper cornucopias.

A cardboard cornucopia
covered with silver paper.

In addition to popcorn, dried apples, and cranberries, there were
chains of peanuts, red haws, and crabapples. Raisins were also put on
strings, but, more often than not, whole clusters of raisins were hung
on the tree, for in those days dried grapes would arrive in the grocery
store still in bunches. From the 1850s on there were numerous accounts of oranges hanging from or borne on the branches of American
Christmas trees.

By the end of the century December candy counters were heaped
with candy for use on the Christmas tree, including commercially
strung, totally unwrapped, strings of brilliantly colored, mouth-

watering hard candies. Temptation also came to children in the form of chains of little pearl-like sugar candies, which could be purchased in many pastel-colored flavors. Although no child ever seemed to know what became of them, sections of these chains often disappeared mysteriously as a youngster sucked on a low-hanging chain while he stood entranced before the other delicious wonders the tree bore.

Old accounts of Christmas trees often list "sugar plums" as ornaments. "Sugar plum" usually meant a multitude of sweets made wholly or principally of sugar rather than a specific fruit. Real sugar plums, however, were occasionally used; these were made by boiling greengage plums in a thick syrup of sugar and cornstarch until they became translucent and preserved. Few things smell better than sugar plums simmering in a pot on a cold December evening, and hung by their stems from colored strings, few decorations could ever have looked more tempting to a Victorian child. Small Seckel pears, apricots, unripe kumquats, and crabapples were also candied for use on the Christmas tree.

Other old accounts of American Christmas trees often speak of "comfits" or "sweetmeats," terms used interchangeably in the nineteenth century for any variety of fruits preserved with sugar. Like "sugar plum," the term "confections" could refer to sugar-crystallized fruit or to any of a great number of candies.

Regardless of what specific name was applied, an abundance of these and other good things to eat were transferred from the kitchen, grocery, and candy shop to the tree. Figurative "clear toys" made from boiled sugar were hung with strings tied around their middle, and candy canes swung from the branches along with chocolates wrapped in gold foil. Tangerines, peanuts, candied coriander seeds, and a profusion of fancy nuts, such as Brazil nuts, usually available only at Christmas time, were balanced in hanging paper cornucopias or placed in doll-sized market baskets or suspended in little net bags cut from circles of folded paper or woven from fine gold string.

Depending on a family's economic circumstances, the types of old-fashioned candy and cookie decorations hung on a Christmas tree could be profuse or modest. In either case, they constituted a visual feast guaranteed to hypnotize children for considerable periods of time. In the 1890s, particularly, it became the fashion for wealthy children to have "tree parties" during the holidays in order to amaze and delight their friends.

One special pleasure afforded by these old-fashioned edible Christmas tree decorations has been all but lost to us today. Traditionally, the tantalizing cookies and sweetmeats that hung on the tree were forbidden fruit, and were supposed to stay in place until the tree was taken down on Twelfth Night, when they could finally be eaten. Therefore, the inevitable final dismantling, so disappointing to today's children, was once an exciting, anticipated, and delicious climax to the Christmas season.

Candy boxes like these were both party favors and tree ornaments.

IV
OLD-TIME ORNAMENTS—
WHO MADE THEM
AND HOW

uring the first years of the twentieth century many Christmas trees were still decorated, at least in part, with edibles. But the old fashion had begun to change in the 1870s with the introduction of the first store-bought ornaments made to be kept from year to year. Late nineteenth-century trees were often magnificently decorated with the best of both worlds. Side by side with the homemade sugary ornaments hung a mind-boggling profusion of store-bought embellishments made of tin, wax, tinsel, cardboard, and glass—a veritable fairyland calculated to overwhelm even a sophisticated child's sense of sight and smell.

Aside from a few commercially made confections, the oldest commercially produced Christmas tree ornaments were made of tin. These were cast from a very soft tin-and-lead alloy by German tinsmiths and by the tin toy makers of Nuremberg, who also cast doll furniture and dolls' dishes from the same soft metal. The earliest tin

55

During the latter part of the nineteenth century color "scrap" prints like this one were common tree ornaments.

Christmas tree ornaments date from the latter part of the eighteenth century. Their popularity on American trees was greatest from 1870 to 1900, by which time they had been superseded by glass ornaments.

Tin ornaments were generally made in geometric shapes such as stars, crosses, and flowers, each multifaceted to catch and reflect the dancing light of nearby candle flames. They usually hung from threads, and were light enough to turn slowly in the air currents created by the burning candles. Today they look crude and dull gray, but when new, they would have been lovely silver reflectors. To increase their effect, a few manufacturers added colorful cut-glass gems, while others were brightly colored with transparent color glazes or were decorated with a lacelike filigree, stamped from the same metal. One of the most ornate of these soft tin ornaments was a butterfly with jeweled wings. Only one of the two sides was finished. The back always showed the impression of the sand or slate molds they were poured into before the face was stamped with a die that gave them the reflective geometric facets.

The next manufactured ornament to make its way to America was made of wax cast in molds by German toy makers. Tiny wax figures of the Holy Child wrapped in silk bunting were recorded here as early as 1800. One Baby Jesus was so small that it lay in half a nutshell decorated with miniature wax roses; another hung suspended in a hollow wax heart. But the most common wax ornaments of the latter half of the nineteenth century were four-inch angels floating in air, through the miracle of thread, hands clasped in prayer. Their wings were made from cardboard, plaster, or spun glass, and their clothes from tinsel or ribbon garlands. Wire halos usually circled above their heads, and by adding a pressed paper crown the angel could easily be turned into the Christ Child.

There were also hollow, molded wax figures, mainly animals, and one example shows a little boy and girl standing on miniature swings.

In the 1870s, before commercially made ornaments became readily available, people made intricate and beautiful ornaments themselves. In a number of Pennsylvania-German communities the hand-making of fancy paper and cardboard ornaments was a fashionable rage. Local competitions and house pride brought out extraordinary ingenuity

Wax ornaments.

ABOVE: A handmade ornament
representing the Christ Child.

as families vied to have the best tree in town. On December 31, 1874, the Carlisle, Pennsylvania, newspaper, *American Volunteer,* described one tree as "loaded with an almost countless number of pretty ornaments, of the latest design, made of variegated cardboard, gold and silver and perforated paper," and another tree as "trimmed with a large variety of handsome card-board ornaments, comprising banners, sleighs, gondolas, chariots, cornucopias, shoes, crosses, fairies, &c."

Magazines, from the 1870s to the 1890s, suggested extremely complicated designs such as four-inch star-shaped candy boxes and tiny boats and carriages that could be intricately traced, cut, and glued. For children, there were simpler patterns for cut paper nets to hold Christmas candy and for bright-colored chains cut and glued with paper strips just like the ones children make today. There were also little men made from the same materials, their head, body, arms, and legs made from paper rings of various sizes.

Prior to 1880 a lot of patience, a little ingenuity, and very little money enabled people to have beautiful tree ornaments, but within a few years it became possible for nearly anyone with the means to have a spectacular tree with very little effort.

Some of the most charming and beautiful ornaments ever manufactured for a Christmas tree are almost unknown today. These were the little silver and gold embossed cardboard "Dresden Christmas tree ornaments," which came in a seemingly endless variety of shapes: dogs, cats, suns, moons, every animal of the barnyard, frogs, turtles, and even alligators. There was a whole sea full of fish, including the European carp, a German Christmas delicacy, and a virtual zoo of exotic creatures, including polar bears, camels, storks, eagles, and peacocks. There were miniature bicycles, skates, sleds, sleighs, trolley cars, sailboats, and ships—from paddle-wheel steamers to ironclads to ocean liners—and also opera glasses, grand pianos, and an entire orchestra of musical instruments.

An astonishing amount of detail could be pressed into these tiny ornaments. (Most were two to three inches high, although a few were as large as six inches.) One could see the hair of a donkey or the wrinkles on an elephant. There were extraordinarily detailed miniature silver sleighs, and gold and silver coronation coaches. One gold carriage was complete with horses, harnesses and all, a coachman on the coach box keeping his feet warm in a sack, and a lady in the carriage, not quite an inch high, with a chenille collar around her neck. There were prancing circus horses with dancing girls balanced on their backs dressed in real silk tutus. A four-inch silver ocean liner had several hundred portholes, all its lifeboats, and tiny cotton puffs of smoke rising from its four smokestacks.

Most of these embossed cardboard ornaments were made between 1880 and 1910. A 1901 German directory lists nine companies specializing in them in the Dresden-Leipzig area alone.

These ornaments were made in several pieces. The animals, for instance, were actually two matching halves, embossed and cut out in the same stamping operation. The process used cardboard, about one thirty-second of an inch thick, dampened to make it slightly elastic. Every tiny elevation in the stamping die, such as a hair in a horse's mane, had to have an equivalent depression in the counter die.

When they were dry, the separate halves were turned over to cottage workers who carried them home for finishing—working for an unbelievably small piecework rate. The two halves of a horse's head, for example, would be carefully glued together, ears were then glued into pre-cut slots, and a bridle made of pressed paper was set in place. Little sleighs or carriages would be upholstered, and silk threads added for the coachman's reins. A two-inch silver steamboat would acquire round paper smokestacks; a rudder and paddle wheel that actually turned had to be pinned on and three-dimensional cabins glued to the deck.

Most "Dresden" ornaments were made of either silver- or gold-faced cardboard. There were some, however, that were painted realistically by artists working for the manufacturers.

Today, despite the fact that the cardboard is surprisingly resistant to time and to handling by generations of children, relatively few examples remain, even though many thousands were produced. Except with German families, they were never as popular in this country as the less expensive glass ornaments imported from Germany at the same time.

In 1880 no one could have predicted the extraordinary success of the glassblowers' creations, which were just beginning to be imported by a handful of American stores. F. W. Woolworth, the great merchant who invented the five-and-ten-cent store, failed to realize

A seven-inch-high Nuremberg angel, made of tin foil, with a china head.

An embossed color print embellished with tinsel rope.

A handmade ornament from Germany.

LEFT: Spun-glass and printed paper ornaments.

the first time he saw glass ornaments that they would soon make a substantial part of his fortune. At the time, however, he had a single variety store in Lancaster, Pennsylvania, and not, as he later admitted, a great deal of foresight when it came to recognizing the potential for glass ornaments:

In the fall of 1880 I went to an importing firm on Strawberry Street, Philadelphia, Meyer & Schoenaman, to buy some toys and about the first thing they did was drag out a lot of colored glass ornaments the like of which I had never seen. "What are those things?" I asked. They explained that these goods were, oh, such fine sellers, but I laughed. "You can't sell me any foolish thing like that," I said. "I don't believe they would sell and most of them would be smashed anyway before there was a chance to sell them." They explained the profit was big enough to offset the breakage, but I was incredulous. It was hard to understand what the people would want of those colored glass things. We argued back and forth a long time and finally the house made me the proposition that it would guarantee the sale, at retail, of twenty five dollars worth of Christmas tree ornaments. "All right," I agreed. "You can send them to me wholly at your own risk."

The goods arrived a few days before Christmas and, with a great deal of indifference, I put them on my counters. In two days they were gone, and I woke up. But it was too late to order any more, and I had to turn away a big demand. The next Christmas season I was on hand early with what I considered a large order, but it was not large enough. They proved to be the best sellers in my store for the holidays.

In February of 1890 Woolworth, who by then had thirteen stores, decided to combine business with pleasure in his first European buying trip. He packed his new Kodak camera and sailed off on the *City of Paris*, the fastest, most luxurious twin-screw steamship of its day. He had a miserable trip. He was seasick and could not eat for five days of the six-day crossing. When he finally reached Lauscha, the little German mountain village where his Christmas tree ornaments had come from, he found the streets ankle deep in March mud. He was taken from one glassblower's house to another to see which of their homemade ornaments he could use, and wrote home that Christmas tree ornaments must be made by "the very poorest class there is in Europe."

The next day in nearby Sonneberg, the wholesale center for the glass ornaments from Lauscha, he was pointed out on every corner and followed about by agents trying to make a sale. That year he bought more than two hundred thousand ornaments.

In the 1890s a different type of glass ornament appeared in American stores. Czechoslovakian glass-bead makers, home workers like their German ornament-making counterparts, strung on a thin wire short lengths of hollow glass tubing and beads of many sizes, shapes, and colors. They made a profusion of geometric shapes—triangles within circles and bright multicolored stars—as well as recognizable objects such as tiny baskets and chandeliers.

Americans of many national backgrounds were buying ornaments for a still relatively small, but ever-growing, number of Christmas trees. They bought not in boxes of a dozen as they would sixty years later, but one or two at a time each Christmas. To accompany their new, shiny glass trinkets, customers turned to shiny tinsel, which further enhanced the excitement of their candle-covered trees.

Rope garlands of tinsel, or lamé, were made by a "secret" process that was originally developed in France for decorating military uniforms and copied by German craftsmen in about 1610. The secret involved drawing a silver-plated copper wire through a series of diamond dies until it was as thin as a human hair. The wire was then passed between two rollers to flatten it and twisted around cording and cut to produce a spiky texture.

Another glittering tinsel product that is still with us today was produced by the tree-loving Germans. "Icicles," first made and sold in Nuremberg in 1878, were thin strips of silver foil designed to drip from decorated boughs like icicles. Immediately a great novelty in America, icicles achieved a lasting success despite the fact that users soon divided into two camps, "hangers" and "throwers." Both factions were usually represented in a single family. Another problem was that cigarette smoke caused the silver icicles to tarnish, so that by the time the tree was taken down the tinsel would often be black and unusable for the following year. Americans soon developed a method of producing lead-foil icicles, which became popular by the 1920s and remained so until a drastic change occurred in the mid 1960s. The U.S. government, concerned by the threat of lead poisoning to children who might swallow tinsel, forced manufacturers to

63

A cardboard yacht with paper sails.

abandon lead foil. Aluminum, which had been tried during World War II, did not drape well, so the manufacturers turned to lightweight silver-colored mylar.

Yet another finishing touch for the tree, "angel's hair," also came from Germany about 1880. Originally, the Germans used it as a rope garland, but Americans began to spread out the strands and to cover the entire tree for a cobweb effect.

In the 1890s tinsel lamé ornaments, commonly but inaccurately known as "lametta," became popular items for the new mail-order

64

A cardboard ship billows cotton "smoke" from its stack.

houses like Sears Roebuck because they were nearly unbreakable. In 1901 the Sears catalogue advertised that its "Christmas tree ornaments are made of tinsel in entirely new and pleasing designs. Much prettier and more durable than the old style of German glass tree ornaments that are so easily broken." Glass ornaments survived the attack, however, and by 1910 Sears was advertising and selling them by mail as well.

The Christmas trees of the 1880s and 1890s reflected the culmination of an interesting phenomenon. Following the Civil War, a scrapbook craze swept America for forty years, reaching its peak in the

65

1890s. Chromolithography, invented in England and adopted by German printers, suddenly put inexpensive full-color pictures within reach of a picture-starved audience. Just as suddenly, every upper- and middle-class woman in Europe and America seemed to be collecting them in scrapbooks. Countless images were painted for and reproduced by this process, which appealed to legions of collectors.

Because of their principal use, these romantic pictures became known as "scraps," and Christmas scraps were placed on many a tree in those days. In the printing process that produced them nineteen or twenty colors were often used, unlike the simplified four-color process of today, so that every tint on a tiny angel's face meant a separate printing. Each subtle color had to be added in exactly the right place, or the effect would not be sharp. After printing, embossing was used to make the features of the angel's face and the feathers of the wings slightly three-dimensional. Scraps were invariably silhouette shapes, which were either handcut or else diecut by the same die that produced their embossed details.

Each Christmas brought a new set of holiday scraps to stationery, variety, and general stores. Nativity scenes were very popular in Victorian America, as were cherubs and beautiful angels with long flowing hair and long flowing dresses, carrying Christmas trees or song books. Old-fashioned Santa Claus figures were dressed, more often than not, in fur-trimmed knee-length coats of blue or green or black like that worn by the German Santa Claus, the *Weihnachtsmann*. These Santas were thin, sad-faced old men more akin to the English Father Christmas, who also appeared on many American trees, than to the still-evolving fat, red-cheeked, red-suited Santa Claus we know today. This happy Santa became the standard image for American children during World War I, when the supply of German scraps and and cards showing the older type was cut off.

By the last decade of the nineteenth century so many scraps were being used to decorate Christmas trees that the German printers began to print the figures with mirror-image reverse sides, which could be pasted together so that the white paper back of the silhouetted scrap would not be visible through the tree. Many scraps were embellished by the addition of tinsel or spun glass or angel's hair.

Other store-bought ornaments for these early trees were made of cotton wool. Like glass ornaments, they were also the products of the

German cottage industry located in the Thuringian mountains. Families of homeworkers cut Santa Claus figures and angels and snow fairies from thin layers of cotton batting and folded and glued them over a wire or cardboard frame. They glued glossy printed faces of Santa or angels or little girls with curly hair to the cotton, and buttons or embossed gold paper wings for the angels. When the little figures were finished, glue was spread on the surface and sprinkled with sparkling glass particles to give a snow-covered effect.

Similar little figures were often made with red or white crepe-paper clothing covering the soft cotton-wool figure inside. Ornament makers would also twist celluloid and cotton wool into the shapes of houses, icicles, oranges, turnips, carrots, mushrooms, and radishes, painting realistic details as a finishing touch. Children loved cotton-wool ornaments because they were usually allowed to play with these inexpensive, unbreakable objects.

Between the 1870s and 1910 many tree ornaments made from bright and shiny wire found their way to this country from Germany, where cottage workers from several villages in the vicinity of Nuremberg specialized in making them. Working with reels of thin wire, which often had already been machine spun into loose cords or crimped to produce a crinkly effect, they hand-tied endless varieties of stars, butterflies, and rosettes.

Other cottagers in Sebnitz, near Dresden, specialized in covering cotton-wool forms with delicate webs made from metallic foil in which small round holes had been stamped out by machine. With these basic materials, they painstakingly fashioned beautiful little zeppelins, sleighs, cottages, wells with buckets, cradles for tiny wax babies, and in one case a gramophone in front of which sat a white wax dog, listening, no doubt, to "his master's voice."

From the 1890s on, many American cities had Japanese stores that sold an array of inexpensive party favors and ornaments. These stores contributed a variety of objects to American trees, but the most popular items for many years were tiny collapsible Japanese lanterns, miniature fans, and brightly colored parasols.

Some of the largest and most unusual decorations that hung on New England trees around the turn of the century were large, realistically painted papier-mâché fishes. Each fish, which could be six to fifteen inches in length, had a large round trap door on one

side, from which would flow a favorite child's favorite candy. They were made during the last years of the nineteenth century by German manufacturers who had perfected the technique of covering molded papier-mâché forms with a thin, smooth, lightweight plasterlike surface that was particularly receptive to finely detailed painting.

The ornament for the top of the tree was always important. Five-inch tin stars and angels with wax heads and long pleated metallic foil skirts, which rustled noisily as they were placed on the topmost point of the tree, were made in Nuremberg at the end of the nineteenth century. At the same time, blown-glass Christmas "treetops" or "points" up to fourteen inches long became available at about five times the cost of a single ball. These were the crowning glories of the German glassblower's art, a graduated series of balls, one above another, with a spike on top and varied reflector surfaces pressed into each ball. The whole complicated ornament was free-blown from a single piece of glass tubing.

Some late-nineteenth-century trees were patriotically topped by small American flags, and many people used little flags on the lower branches. Tinsel-entwined paper shields decorated with the Stars and Stripes were also very popular.

But beyond a doubt, the most exciting top for many an old-fashioned candle-lit tree was the big wax angel, often suspended by a fine wire just above the tree as if hovering over it on spun-glass wings. These angels were wax-covered papier-mâché figures made in Nuremberg in sizes ranging from four to eleven inches high. As the heat of the candles rose to meet the little angel, it would revolve, turning slowly, first one way and then the other. To adults and children alike, it didn't take much imagination to believe that there was a real angel flying above the tree.

The problem of how to hang ornaments brought forth a variety of solutions, some of which lasted and some of which did not. The old, heavy glass ornaments from Germany were sealed by and hung from a cork glued into the stem, but in the 1880s these same heavy ornaments were given a round, flat brass top, decorated like the end of a Victorian curtain rod. Wires tied to sticks of wood and accordion-pleated cardboard hangers that unfolded inside the balls were also tried. (During World War II, when metal caps were not available, American ornament makers had to go back to that solution.) In the

69

A papier-mâché candy box made in Germany c. 1900.

1880s rubber strings were tried and abandoned. The characteristic old "crinkled" wire found as the hanger on many old ornaments dates only from 1913.

In the 1890s little metal caps with two holes through the top for thread were glued to the top of each ornament by the glassblowers' wives or children. Like threading a needle, thread or thin wire had to be pushed painstakingly through the holes and tied in a loop. Today's metal cap with its spring clip dates from about the turn of the century, but unfortunately, the exact date of its invention and other details of this simple and long-lasting device have been obscured by time.

One of the great inventions in Christmas tree history, Christmas tree hooks, was announced in a wholesaler's catalogue in 1892 like this:

It is a well known fact, that heretofore it has taken the best part of Christmas Eve to trim a tree by tying strings or threads to the trinkets, and then tying these to the tree, thus taking about 2 to 3 hours of one person's time and labor to trim a tree with 100 articles. With these hooks, the same number can be applied in less than half an hour.

No description of the ornaments that once hung on the Christmas tree would be complete without mention of two additional items, both basically toys that became applied to the tree. In the latter half of the nineteenth century many small wooden toys, including little birdhouses, soldiers, and dolls, hung from the branches of many American Christmas trees. Carved, sanded, and brightly painted, they were usually the product of toy-making woodcarvers from the Erzgebirge and Berchtesgaden mountain regions of Germany. Celluloid toys and miniature dolls made especially to adorn the Christmas tree were first made around 1875 by a manufacturer in Mannheim, Germany. Unfortunately, celluloid was highly flammable, and these ornaments were blamed for many tree fires, having been ignited by a nearby candle on the tree. Despite the danger, they remained common Christmas tree decorations during the early years of this century.

The Christmas of 1908 saw the first three-inch red honeycombed paper bells on American trees, made by the now-defunct Paper Novelty Products Company of New York. The larger version of that company's bell has remained a Christmas classic for sixty years. In

A miniature Victorian house conceals a candy box in its base.

A four-inch-high figure of *Weihnachtsmann,* the German Santa Claus, who carried both toys and switches.

A gold cardboard cigar and a little tennis racket were ornaments designed to hold candy.

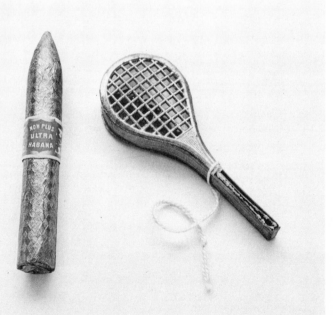

the 1930s, the same firm introduced the red and green crushed crepe-paper ropes that have decorated innumerable trees, store windows, and classrooms ever since.

For Christmas 1914, after the outbreak of World War I, German ornaments were still fairly plentiful in America. But before the next season the Allies had put an embargo on German products. Christmas ornaments could be had by people willing to pay what storekeepers asked for them, but by 1916 the stock left over from previous years had been exhausted. The shelves were bare.

In 1918 the first attempts at American-made ornaments appeared in toy stores, the hasty product of a few American toy makers. Only round balls were available for the tree and they were crude and less than color-fast. *Scientific American* reported the following year that "even the children noticed the difference and wanted to know what was the matter with Santa Claus?"

Within three years a better, more polished product was available, including a few twisted and irregular-shaped ornaments; but American makers never mastered the various fruit, doll, and Santa Claus shapes at which the German glassblowers excelled. Nor did they overcome the problem of a perceptible brownish tint on what were supposed to be their bright red balls.

Consequently, Germany had little trouble regaining its market in the early 1920s. Most of the American production fell by the wayside, unable to compete with either the German quality or its prices.

Finally, in 1938 the Paper Novelty Products Company bought rights from Disney and under their Double-Glo trade name sold decorations made by glassblowers in Brooklyn, New York. The ornaments depicted Snow White and the Seven Dwarfs. These figures were crude and the glass was heavy in comparison to German ornaments, but they deserve to be remembered as the first handblown figurative ornaments to be produced in quantity in America. There was no attempt to hand paint the figures realistically: Snow White was dipped in white paint, and the dwarfs were just as simply lacquered in bright colors, a different one for each.

During the Depression another enterprising American manufacturer started making cardboard ornaments for the Christmas tree, producing little wagons, baby carriages, and drums stamped from lightweight, bright-colored cardboard sprinkled with a frosting of clear, shiny crystals. Unlike their German predecessors, the Dresden ornaments, these cardboard ornaments were neither detailed nor embossed, but their small size and bright colors gave them a certain toylike charm.

In New York City in the late 1930s, Max Eckardt, an importer of German Christmas tree ornaments since 1907, could see by events in Germany that soon he was likely to be out of the ornament business again, as he had been during World War I. So he set about to make America the world's number-one glass-ornament maker in only a few years. Together with Bill Thompson of F. W. Woolworth he was instrumental in convincing Corning Glass to take up the mass production of machine-made Christmas tree balls.

Eckardt was born in Oberlind in 1890, in the forest-covered, mountainous area of Germany that was economically dominated by crafts related to the making of toys. Since Oberlind was twenty miles from Lauscha, the birthplace of the glass Christmas tree ball, he grew up with some knowledge of his future trade. After he left school, his first job was with a wooden toy manufacturer in Sonneberg. However, he soon found that all the important German toy firms were family held and promotion to top management would be long and slow. Like many other young men from the area, he decided to emigrate to America.

Upon arriving in New York he went to work for a toy salesman who also imported ornaments from Lauscha. In the early 1920s he discussed partnership with Louis Marx, another young immigrant who went on to make a fortune in tin toys, but nothing ever came of the talks. Nevertheless, by 1926 Eckardt owned Strauss/Eckardt, and the same year he built a large factory with his brother Ernst in Oberlind. That partnership was called Gebruder Eckardt (Brothers Eckardt), and they specialized in wooden toys and glass Christmas tree ornaments. Eckardt's American firm was renamed Max Eckardt and Sons after World War II, and their toys and dolls were discontinued as his business became America's largest importer and manufacturer of Christmas tree ornaments.

In the 1930s Eckardt spent part of each year in Germany, and followed the political situation there with a sense of foreboding. By 1937 he was convinced Hitler had Germany on a collision course with war.

Cardboard champagne bottles that
decorated American trees in the
1890s.

BELOW: Embossed cardboard "Dresden"
ornaments. While most of these decorations
were made of shiny silver or gold cardboard,
a few, like these, were realistically painted.

Japanese paper ornaments.

Czechoslovakian glass ornaments.

He knew that a number of Lauscha glassblowers had, over the years, come to the United States to work for Corning Glass. He went to Corning, New York, to talk to some of them about his idea of starting an American-based glass-ornament business. While he was there an idea was born that would move the ornament capital of the world from Lauscha, Germany, to a Corning plant in Wellsboro, Pennsylvania.

Corning held exclusive patents to a "ribbon" glassblowing machine developed for the manufacture of electric light bulbs. The machine could blow two thousand light bulbs a minute, and its production rate could easily be increased. Eckardt reasoned that if it could make a light bulb it ought to be able to blow a Christmas tree ball.

In 1939 Woolworth's joined Eckhardt in predicting correctly that war would soon cut off imports from Germany. It offered to place a huge order if Corning could successfully adopt its bulb machine to

ornaments. In December of 1938 Corning had already begun to experiment with ornament molds. Early in December of 1939 the first 235,000 Corning blown and machine-lacquered ornaments were shipped to Woolworth's. The Corning machines could make more ornaments in a single minute than a German cottage glassblower could make in a day.

The following year big cartons of clear glass balls were shipped to Eckardt's new decorating plant in New Jersey, where they were silvered inside, lacquered, and hand decorated.

The new venture was only two years old when the United States entered World War II. The war-time shortages eventually made it impossible for Corning to get either lacquer or silver for the decorating, and soon metal for the little caps and hangers was also unavailable. Eckardt, whose decorating firm now produced ornaments under the trade name "Shiny Brite," continued throughout the war to decorate ornaments. However, in 1944, when he could no longer get silver or lacquer, he decorated the clear glass balls only with thin painted stripes in pastel colors. First folded cardboard hangers and later glued-on cardboard caps were used to replace the metal caps.

Following the war Shiny Brite became the biggest ornament company in the world. In the late 1940s and early 1950s Eckardt had four plants in New Jersey lacquering and painting the new ornaments that were placed on American trees. The reason for four small plants instead of one big one was the explosive nature of the silver nitrate and the lacquer used. Despite the fact that nobody could smoke in any of the factories and that every possible precaution was taken, Shiny Brite had a number of small fires and one very bad one.

In the late 1960s Corning returned for the first time since the early war years to decorating ornaments in its own plants while continuing to supply blanks to Shiny Brite and other finishers. In one way or another, Corning still produces most of the glass ornaments made in America.

A handmade German ornament.

A dye-cut paper print.

V
LAUSCHA–THE TOWN
THAT INVENTED THE
CHRISTMAS TREE BALL

ixty miles north of Nuremberg, Germany, high in the Thuringian mountains, and deep in a forest of 80-foot-tall Christmas trees, lies the village of Lauscha. Its ornamentally decorated slate-covered houses perch on steep streets nestled at the bottom of a narrow mountain valley. In the 1930s Lauscha looked like a storybook German town.

At that time ninety-five percent of the glass ornaments on American Christmas trees came from the immediate vicinity of this little town. During the 1840s Lauscha was the birthplace of a cottage industry that supplied virtually all blown-glass Christmas-tree ornaments until just before World War I, when a company in Vienna began to copy the Lauscha ornaments. In the 1920s and 1930s Polish, Czechoslovakian, and Japanese glassblowers did the same, but, until World War II, Lauscha remained the ornament maker for American trees.

By 1930 approximately two thousand homes and six thousand people in the immediate vicinity of Lauscha were engaged in the

81

Three old ornaments which show the fascination of the German ornament makers with the idea of flight.

A bear carrying a broom.

A postcard view of Lauscha
in the Thuringian mountains.

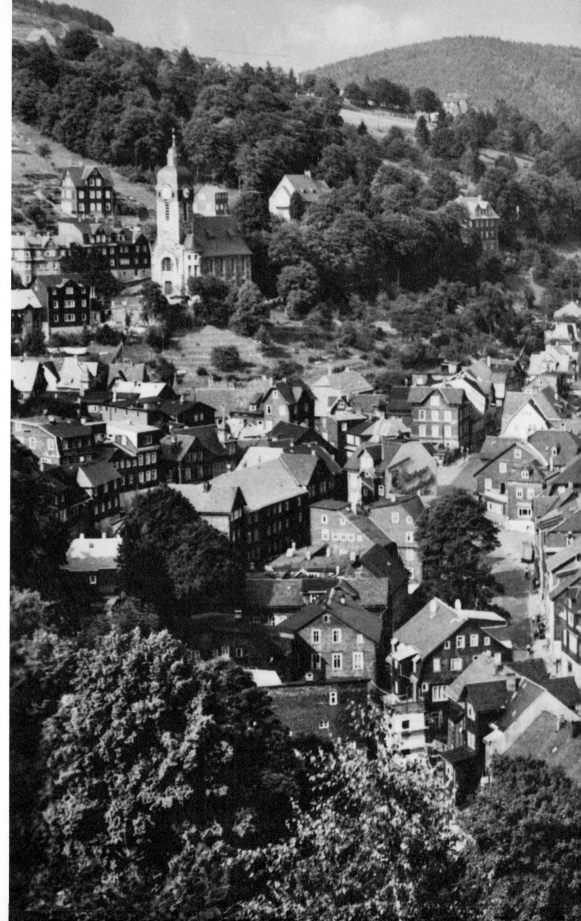

ornament trade. Their craft had remained almost entirely unchanged since before the turn of the century.

An ornament maker's home was his factory, his wife and everyone in the family were its staff and production line. He had a small *werkstatt,* or workshop, attached to his home just as many Americans have an attached garage.

Blowing ornaments was hot work. Sitting all day over a flame hot enough to melt glass was sweaty work, winter or summer. A man needed fourteen or fifteen glasses of beer a day to replace the liquid he lost. If you dropped in on a glassblower unexpectedly in those days, you would probably find him perched on a high stool, bent over his bench, clad only in his long underwear with a pair of brown leather slippers on his feet.

Behind him, as far from the flame of the Bunsen burner as possible, were drums of lacquer and a hot pot of silvering solution, the latter a combination of silver nitrate, quicklime, and milk sugar. Every glassblower had his own family formula, which he believed was better than anyone else's.

His wife handled the tedious job of silvering the inside of the ornaments he was blowing. She filled each newly blown ball one-quarter full with the solution, and then shook it. To get the silvering to spread evenly, she would dip it in hot water several times. Since the shaking action was difficult, boring work, she developed a method of holding several in one hand with the six-inch stems or "pikes" sticking out between her fingers like a porcupine. But that was the only shortcut possible. Uneven silvering showed even after the ornament had been lacquered, and there was little chance the wholesaler would buy these ornaments.

After the coating was complete, she poured the excess solution out into a basin where the silver would be chemically separated and used again. Then she slipped the pikes over nails protruding from long boards and hung the ornaments up to dry, hanging in rows from the ceiling rafters over the stove.

The following morning the board was taken down, at which point most of the shiny silver ornaments were dipped in various colored lacquers in the workshop. The family grew so used to the overpowering smell of lacquer that they hardly noticed it, but some never became accustomed to it. F. W. Woolworth remembered being ap-

84

palled by the odor in 1890, and an importer who used to visit the village in the 1930s once said that, as you approached in a car, you could tell one hundred feet away that you had come to a glassblower's cottage.

After dipping, the ornaments were returned to their nails, positioned so that the excess lacquer would run off down the pike without spoiling the even finish on the ball.

All members of the family helped with the painted trimmings that decorated many of the ornaments. When the paint was dry, the oldest child was entrusted with scoring the pikes with a small blade coated with an abrasive. Once scored, the pike broke off easily and cleanly. Then the youngest child was given the job of putting the little metal caps on.

Working eight to fifteen hours a day, often six days a week, a family could make from three hundred to six hundred ornaments a day.

Glassmaking began in Lauscha in the 1590s when religious persecution in the German province of Swabia forced little groups of Protestant glassmakers to leave their homes. They were drawn to the Thuringian mountains by an abundance of wood, sand, and limestone, the necessary ingredients for their craft. In 1597, with the permission of the Duke of Coburg, they built a small cooperative glass factory in Lauscha.

Other glass works followed. The village became a center for products such as drinking glasses and bulls-eye window glass. For the next few centuries, the glass was sold by peddlers making their rounds, sometimes several hundred miles from Lauscha.

As more and more glassmakers were drawn to this new center of their trade, local authorities decided to limit the building of new factories because of the heavy demand the furnaces were making on the wood supply from local forests. As a result, some glassblowers set up small workshops in their homes.

In the middle of the eighteenth century some of these craftsmen began to make glass beads. The glassblower would first ignite a cup of turnip oil, increasing the flame by forcing air into the oil through a tube from his mouth. He would then melt the end of a small, hollow, glass rod in the flame and blow into it until he got a bubble of the right size. Hardened beads of glass were cut from the end of the rod, coated on the inside with lead or zinc, and filled with wax.

85

Later, the constant work of feeding the flame with air was somewhat simplified by the use of an inflated goatskin bag which the glassblower pressed under his arm as he worked, like a bagpipe. This innovation was eventually replaced by an even easier knee-operated bellows under the workbench.

One large family named Greiner specialized in beads, and at one time its members almost singlehandedly supplied the jewelry and millinery trades throughout Europe. Production of glass beads continued to grow until the demands of fashion made glass beads into Lauscha's number-one business.

But beginning in 1845 glassblowers in Bohemia began to produce beads superior to those produced in Lauscha. First the Bohemians developed a bead blown into a porcelain mold that produced an etched effect. Then, in 1857, they devised a silver-nitrate solution that gave their beads a brilliant, mirrorlike, silver luster.

Almost overnight Lauscha lost most of its bead market to the competition. Hard times prevailed until a Lauscha glassmaker, Louis Greiner-Schlotfeger, descended from the original bead-blowing Greiners, succeeded in duplicating the Bohemians' silver formula, thus saving what was left of the town's bead business.

He also blew thick-walled glass balls, which he silvered with his shiny new mirror solution. This type of glass object had been made in Lauscha since the 1820s by glassblowers who amused themselves by seeing how large a bubble of glass they could blow. They were known as *kugels* and many had been "silvered" inside with lead or zinc to give them a reflective effect. Some were fastened to wooden crowns and hung from the ceiling during the Christmas season, and it was not long before the tree-decorating Germans decided that these small *kugels* looked well on the Christmas tree. The first written record of glass Christmas tree balls being produced does not appear until 1848, when "six dozen of Christmas tree ornaments in three sizes" was recorded in a Lauscha glassblower's book.

Among the oldest Christmas tree balls made in Lauscha were those called *schecken*, which means spotted or dappled. The same ornaments are also known by the musical name of *plumbum*, pronounced plume-boom), meaning lead. A small puddle of hot lead was dripped into a round or egg-shaped ball. With a quick twist of his wrist the glassblower produced a wide, rough lead stripe, which spiraled at a 45-degree angle about two and a half times around the inside of a clear glass ornament. *Plumbum* were usually completed by covering the rest of the inside of the glass with red, green, or yellow wax, which made the lead appear a brighter silver color. Golden *plumbum* were made with yellow-brown glass that, when striped with lead and coated with wax, appeared to be made of gold.

The production of Christmas tree ornaments began at a good time for the depressed economy of Lauscha, which was struggling to replace its lost bead business with new items such as glass marbles, glass toys, laboratory glass, and glass eyes.

In 1867 a gas works was built in Lauscha. For the first time the glassblowers had a steady, very hot, easily adjustable gas flame, which would make possible large, thin-walled bubbles of glass.

Louis Greiner-Schlotfeger perfected a paper-thin, four-inch version of the old heavy *kugel,* and he is said to have discovered the idea in 1870 for molded glass ornaments by blowing a bubble of glass into a pine-cone-shaped cookie mold. Soon the glassblowers in his small firm were producing glass pine cones, as well as blown-glass apples and pears and crystal icicles for tree ornaments. At first, he sold them through the old *rafftrageir,* peddlers with pack baskets, but in a short time they were being exported to America.

Before many years went by, most artisans in Lauscha were blowing ornaments of one sort or another. A report from the Chamber of Commerce of Sonneberg, a trading center a dozen miles down the valley from Lauscha, spoke of a growing demand for Christmas tree ornaments during the years 1878 to 1882. In 1889 it was noted that ornaments had become Lauscha's principal product. Buyers for American stores, including F. W. Woolworth, began making ornament-buying trips to Lauscha at the same time they were buying toys and dolls in the nearby Nuremberg and Sonneberg areas. The making of ornaments totally dominated the life of Lauscha and would soon take over the neighboring village of Steinheid as well.

In 1902 M. Wyerman, a German economist, wrote:

If in the evening you ride in the train from the toy city, Sonneberg, slowly up the Steinach Valley, which is getting more and more

A blown-glass bird with spun-glass tail and wings.

narrow, and you approach Lauscha some 2000 feet above sea-level, already in the first houses you can see one or more bluish lights, which soon you find spreading like glow-worms all over the village. They are the small jets of the lamp blowers, the home workers of the glass industry, who especially during the season (June to the beginning of November) work until late at night.

By 1890 the Lauscha glassblowers had perfected the use of *formsachen* (molds) in their work. The top and bottom halves of a mold were glued to a set of iron hand tongs, a heavy tool that usually rested on something in front of the glassblower while he worked. By the 1930s he had developed a handmade iron device with a steel spring, which was clamped upright on his workbench. This both held the mold at the right height and allowed him to open and close it by means of a foot pedal.

Blowing an ornament in a mold was a time-consuming but fairly simple operation. Reheating the closed end of a thin tube of glass that he had just sealed over his Bunsen burner, he blew a bubble the same shape and only a little smaller than the ornament he was about to make. Quickly he would place the still orange-hot molten bubble in the bottom half of the mold and close the top, leaving only the blowing end of the tube protruding through a small hole left for it. Working fast, before the glass could cool and always blowing downward into

ABOVE: A trumpet, painstakingly blown and twisted from a straw-like rod of glass.

The glass bird with a berry in its beak and the three baby birds in the nest were blown into molds; the stork was free-blown.

Three Santa figures; the one with the long coat is the German *Weihnachtsmann*.

the mold, he expanded the thin glass bubble inside to fill the mold. After only a few seconds he opened the mold and a bird or acorn or some other recognizable shape emerged.

The growing need for molds brought a new type of craftsman to Lauscha. A mold maker was primarily a skilled artist or doll maker who could mold anything the glassblowers or the American importers asked for. His original wood or, more likely, clay model was called a "motherform." Once he had made a Santa Claus figure, for instance, he would grease it with goose or pig fat and cast it one half at a time in a plaster-of-Paris-like material, which quickly absorbed the extreme heat of the molten glass and cooled it without itself shrinking or expanding.

Over the years thousands of different molds were produced. The glassblowers of Lauscha reproduced every conceivable fruit and vegetable—from apples, pears, and oranges to corn, beets, and potatoes and even several different kinds of pickle. Dogs, cats, monkeys, and bears abounded, along with clowns and storybook characters, and religious figures, including the Christ Child, angels, and the Christian symbol, the fish. There was a whole little village of different glass houses and churches to be hung on the tree, and also utilitarian objects like purses and pipes.

The pine cone was an often repeated theme. Other favorite designs were Santas, birds, nuts, flowers, clusters of grapes, and musical instruments such as drums and violins. Innumerable geometric designs were also made, most of them intricate and ingenious variations on a basic ball shape. The imagination and skill of the designers were prodigious.

A single design, such as an acorn or a tulip or a Santa Claus figure, was often made in three different sizes. Large or small, they were exact replicas, as exact as the mold maker working in clay could produce.

Today only a very large collection of old ornaments can give an idea of the seemingly limitless number of molds that were made between the 1880s and 1939. There is no way of knowing how many different designs there may have been, though five thousand might serve as a conservative estimate. During those years it was the natural desire of the artisans as well as the wholesalers and retailers to offer something new each year that might stimulate business. At the same time there was pressure to continue to make the old designs that sold well. Hundreds of designs came and went—many of the rarest of them today were probably produced for a single season by a single man.

One of the most enduring of patterns was the bird with a spun-glass tail, which originally hung from a delicate glass hook protruding from the back or head. By 1900, however, the glassblowers had borrowed the clip from the clip-on candleholder of the period and the birds acquired either one or two metal spring legs, which were soldered to the clip base before being glued into indentations in the bird's belly.

Many people remember or still have the fragile glass bird from Grandmother's tree, but few have ever seen the many different kinds of birds that were originally made. In addition to a number of small birds native to Germany, unidentifiable to most Americans, there were

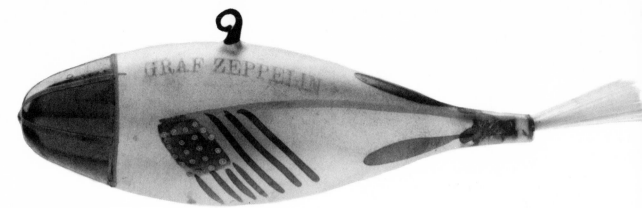

A Graf Zeppelin ornament made for American trees.

A glass cuckoo clock with a paper clock face.

Tiny houses and churches were popular ornaments which were made in innumerable patterns.

This "plumbum" ornament from the Smithsonian Institution is unusual in that lead was dripped down the inner walls rather than swirled in a spiral.

An imperious blue dog.

cockatoos, parrots, and owls. Regardless of species, most birds, including a peacock, had a two-inch tail made of hair-fine strands of spun glass. Those that didn't could boast a crinkly wire tail.

Many Lauscha-made ornaments reveal the playfulness of the delightful imaginative minds behind the creation. There are glass boats with cardboard sails and tinsel-wire rigging that look as if they were designed to sail over the moon in a child's story. One ornament maker's flight of fancy produced a pear with a face like the man in the moon. Someone else made a dog wearing a white collar and necktie. And another beautiful old ornament was a four-inch-high snowman with three children dancing around his base.

The snowman, like others of the oldest paper-thin glass balls still surviving, was not silvered inside, but merely dipped in matte lacquer and painted. Others, like the pear and an exquisitely modeled little girl's head, were silvered and then sprayed with matte lacquers to achieve a subtle luminous glow impossible without the mirror surface inside. Old-fashioned matte lacquer was made by doctoring shiny lacquer with home formulas that usually included starch.

Imaginatively conceived and lovingly made, many of these ornaments. with their naturalistic motifs transcended their commercial origins and deserve to be recognized as an important form of German folk art.

Klausmann, as Lauscha knew the Santa Claus figures, were always fashioned without legs, stopping in a rounded base at the end of Santa's coat. Santas from Lauscha almost always carried little Christmas trees along with a bag of toys. In the 1930s Czechoslovakian glassblowers imitated the German figures, but curiously enough, they never showed Santa Claus carrying a Christmas tree.

Some of the molds reflected current events of the period. A wave of enthusiasm for balloon ascensions gripped both Germany and the United States in the 1890s. This excitement was reflected in many balloon-shaped ornaments, including versions with wire-tinseled mesh ropes, embossed lithographic cutouts of angels, and Santa Claus riding in the balloon's gondola. The world's new fascination, motoring, was also reflected on Christmas trees of the 1920s when a small automobile of the period was reproduced as an ornament.

Two of the most popular comic-strip characters of the early years of this century were "Foxy Grandpa" and "Happy Hooligan," each of whom was quickly immortalized in glass by the German ornament makers. When the Theodore Roosevelt "Teddy Bear" craze gripped America, many teddy-bear ornaments suddenly appeared.

Likewise, when the Graf Zeppelin made news by flying around the world from Germany and across America in 1929, a zeppelin-shaped ball with a spun-glass tail was made to hang on German and American trees. For the export market, an American flag was painted on both sides.

Some shapes were produced without molds. Glassblowers pushed and pulled a free-blown bubble into a different shape while it was hot, using the simplest of wooden tools and an asbestos-covered leather glove. They blew tiny teapots and annealed delicate spouts and handles to them. In the same manner they made trumpets, lyres, anchors, and butterfly bodies to which glass silk wings were attached. The toadstool, considered a sign of good luck in Germany, was also a common object made without a mold. Trumpets that could be blown and bells that rang required the utmost craftsmanship and could be mastered only after about five years' experience. One master craftsman produced perhaps the ultimate free-blown Christmas tree ornament when he blew, twisted, and coaxed a thin rod of glass into a delicate eight-inch stork to stand majestically on a Christmas tree branch.

Ornaments with concave reflectors in them would begin as free-blown ornaments. The glassblower would then heat one side over his flame, and with a little plaster mold of the reflector shape he wanted, would carefully press the design to a depth pleasing to the eye. Today most reflectors are geometric, but originally they also included pictures such as churches or flowers.

Some ornament makers embellished their ornaments by adding wire tinsel, cotton batting, or silk-thread tassels. One of the most beautiful—and difficult—variations was hand wrapping the crinkled silver or gold wire that was always done for balloons and airships and many other turn-of-the-century ornaments. In the case of a balloon with a basket, since the top was bigger than the bottom, wrapping evenly was something that only a relatively few craftsmen could accomplish. At the end of the production line, it was usually the grandmother in the family who patiently added the wire tinsel.

In addition to their customary lacquering and painting, Lauscha craftsmen varied the decoration of some of their ornaments with several simple techniques. Parts of some balls were dipped into or painted with glue and then sprinkled with tiny chips of crushed glass to give a glistening effect. A glimmering variation on the process substituted tiny beads of glass. A more sophisticated technique, which would originally have been a secret closely guarded by the family that developed it, involved etching the glass surface with fluoride. This gave the surface of the ornaments a subtle frosted appearance reminiscent of a window on a frosty morning.

Some glassblowers specialized in free-blowing the nine-, twelve-, and fourteen-inch "tree tops" shaped like the spike on a Prussian officer's helmet. That was another difficult feat, accomplished with a little stick and a great deal of acrobatic turning of the glassblower's head. If you have ever seen a tree top that isn't absolutely straight, it does not mean that the glassblower was incompetent. Probably he was getting tired after a long day, or perhaps he had a "Monday head," as the glassblowers described a hangover induced by too much beer on Sunday evening.

Sunday afternoon, when weather permitted, the ornament makers fielded a soccer team against a team of doll makers or truckers. After the game they would return to one of their beer halls, which were their equivalent of guild halls. Here they boasted exorbitantly about how many ornaments they had made that week. These long Sunday-evening get-togethers usually resulted in a large consumption of beer and wurst.

Friday was traditionally the wife's day out of the house. This was go-to-market day for the ornaments, which were packed in a very large wicker basket, which the wife carried on her back knapsack fashion to the wholesaler or "collector." The rectangular basket was suspended below her waist and towered a foot and a half above her head, for although the ornaments were inherently light, they were bulky. Depending on whether she had daughters big enough to help her, she might make two or three trips by railroad to Sonneberg, where the warehouses of the American buyers were located. To save a trip, some women loaded themselves until they looked like enormous black birds waddling down the street. Across the basket on their backs they tied a wide bundle of additional ornaments, sometimes as broad as the woman was tall. While in town, she would have her get-together with the other wives over sausages and beer at the big *brauhaus*.

Monday was the usual day for the men to go to town to buy their supplies, but in the 1930s the system began to change. It was more efficient to have the collector they worked for supply the glass rods and the five-gallon cans of lacquer, delivering these materials by truck. In some cases the collector's truck also began to call for the big baskets of ornaments. Woolworth, Kresge, Kress, and America's largest importer, Max Eckardt, all had warehouses in the Sonneberg area, and glassblowers now worked for only one company.

In the latter part of the nineteenth century the glassblowers were greatly exploited. From the beginning, ornament distribution had been handled as a sideline by book publishers in Sonneberg, who served as middlemen between the glassblowers and foreign buyers. A publisher found the buyers, found out what they wanted, and finally made contracts for the individual glassblowers.

Since the publisher's first loyalty was always to the big buyer rather than to the individual ornament makers, and much of the year the artisans needed the work at any price, the piecework price was usually very low. Lauscha knew a lot of lean months and hard times.

But eventually the makers gained a little bargaining power as independent collectors became managers of fifty to one hundred workshops each. When the American buyers began warehousing in Germany, the year-round production of ornaments became possible, ending the feast-or-famine existence that had long been a part of the ornament maker's life.

The finished boxes of ornaments moved from Sonneberg by rail to the ports in the north of Germany. Steamship lines gave very good rates to America's ornament importers, for Christmas tree balls made perfect "top cargo." After the ship's hold had been filled almost to its weight limit with heavy cargo, the big, light crates of ornaments could be used to fill up the hold.

The hot, hard, but somehow satisfying way of life for the glassblowers was totally disrupted by the war in 1939. After the war the border placed Lauscha ten miles inside East Germany and thus lost the valuable American market.

In 1949, in an effort to help the West German economy, the U.S. Government sent Max Eckardt and one of his sons to try to reestablish an ornament industry in Europe. There were a number of Lauscha refugees in the Coburg area, only about twenty miles from their old

A cat playing a fiddle with a German student's hat on its head, and a happy glass clown.

homes, and there was still a need for the fragile, detailed, handblown, hand-decorated, figurative ornaments that could never be made by machine.

Between 1950 and the early 1960s about twenty percent of America's ornaments were again imported from Germany. But times, economic conditions, and old age took their toll. A school for glass-blowers was started in Neustadt, West Germany, only a mile from the border, and for a few years the old Lauscha men trained eight to fifteen young glassblowers a year. But the work was difficult and as the West German economy boomed, there was too much "quick money" to be made elsewhere. One could drive a truck or work in a plant, with benefits including medical insurance and pensions, and higher wages than the old-fashioned craft could pay. If an ornament maker's son wanted to follow his father's trade, he soon felt economic pressures from his peers and his family. Few young girls in the new Germany dreamed of working as hard as had the cottage workers' wives.

During the years immediately following World War II, the iron curtain was somewhat porous and about six hundred glassblowers and their families moved to the West by sneaking through the woods on dark nights. Among those who stayed in Lauscha a ten-year-long black-market operation in Christmas tree ornaments developed. On foggy nights Lauscha men stealthily carried baskets, old suitcases, and bundles of their fragile glass ornaments rolled in tablecloths to silent border meetings, where the ornaments were slipped under the barbed-wire fence. In return they got razor blades, coffee, cigarettes, and other commodities hard to obtain in the eastern zone.

Within the 1960s times improved on both sides of the border but, East or West, the ornament makers continued to have little reward beyond the satisfaction of their work. Today in West Germany fewer people make ornaments by hand with every passing year.

In Lauscha only a few old men, too old to work regularly, still blow ornaments in their homes, while others handblow them on the production line at the government factory in Lauscha. They still use a number of their old molds but very few of the ornaments find their way to America.

In a few years there will be no more home production in Lauscha, the home of the shining and imaginative glass ornaments that delighted children and adults alike for so many old-fashioned Christmases.

Candles mounted on wooden hoops were used to decorate the trees in this German print of 1850.

VI
CANDLES—
HANDLE WITH CARE

he scent of a candle-lit tree was as much a part of Christmas as the smell of a turkey roasting in the oven. A Michigan woman remembers waiting at the top of the stairs with her brothers and sisters while her father went down early Christmas morning to light the tree in the quiet, dark room. No child was tempted to peek because none wanted to spoil the effect by seeing the tree until it was ablaze with all its candles. As the glimmer of the first candles grew into a glow in the room below, up the stairs wafted the incredible mixture of the scent of burning candles together with the aroma of pine tree, heightened by its proximity to the heat of the candles. Some families lit their tree first on Christmas morning, while others saved and savored the excitement until Christmas night.

Today, in order to appreciate the true beauty of a tree with candles lighted, it is necessary to imagine its effect in an otherwise totally darkened room.

The typical old-fashioned parlor had double wooden or curtain-covered doors which would be shut, leaving the rest of the family waiting impatiently in the hall outside while Father lit the candles. The children's hearts would beat fast with excitement. After five minutes (which always seemed like fifteen), when at last he threw open the doors, the effect was breathtakingly beautiful. Without fail, the sight drew a simultaneous chorus of "Ah" from everyone rushing to surround the tree.

The desire to put candles on a Christmas tree grew out of an age-old tradition. In Christian symbolism candles represented Christ, and for more than one thousand years in European churches and homes, candles were lighted on Christmas Eve to welcome the Christ Child.

The candle-lit Christmas tree probably originated as the decorated fir tree of Alsace, spreading eastward and northward, met the evergreen-decorated, pyramid-shaped candlestand somewhere in Germany. We do not know just where or when. But we do know that an unlighted tree and a bough-covered, candle-lit pyramid stood side by side in some German rooms one hundred years after the first candle-lit trees were reported by Liselotte von der Pfaz about 1660 in the south of Germany.

For the next 140 years most of the very few accounts that can be found refer simply to the presence of a lighted tree without telling how it was lighted. Light was not necessarily produced by candles, for in Germany at that time wax was expensive. Most people used various forms of tallow lights in their homes, and we know that some Christmas trees were lighted with a wick floating in oil held in half a nutshell.

One form of candle used on early Christmas trees was a long, thin taper flexible enough to be tied around a branch. When thicker candles were used, they were painstakingly tied or wired to the bough.

Weiss tanne are uniquely shaped fir trees, indigenous to Germany, where they are commonly used as Christmas trees. They have wide, empty spaces along the trunk between rows of boughs, which grow like spokes on a wheel. Those spaces are ideal for candles, and so the shape of the *tanne* gave rise to two old-fashioned candleholding devices in Germany that could never be transferred to the anatomy of American evergreens. In 1817 an English traveler in Germany witnessed "Three fir trees encircled BY HOOPS OF FIRE." He had seen graduated sets of lightweight wooden rings that rested horizontally on the boughs with small candles placed every few inches around them. The second device, also practical only on a *tanne,* was a candle bracket mounted on the end of a long metal rod that could be screwed into the trunk of the tree.

Old prints from the middle of the nineteenth century show candleholders attached to branches with small dishes to catch dripping wax. An adaptation of this idea, developed in the 1880s, was a small tin dish with a crimped edge, which was attached to the tree branch by means of a needlelike tack, the other end of which skewered the candle. But they were not easy to apply near the end of a bough, and the weight of the candle gave them a tendency to lean in one direction or the other, sometimes dangerously so. Even a slightly leaning candle often dripped wax onto the tree and ornaments, or onto the floor beneath the tree.

These problems had brought forth a seemingly ingenious solution —the counterweighted candleholder, invented by Charles Kirchhof in Newark, New Jersey. A U.S. patent was issued to Kirchhof for his invention on December 24, 1867. His candleholder eliminated the need to wire or skewer a candle and cup to a branch, but simply hooked over the branch and held its candle perfectly upright with a counterbalancing weight suspended on a wire beneath the candle. The weight, made of unfired clay, was a ball the size of a cherry. These balls were usually painted and added their own decorative spot of color to the tree. By 1878 a German wholesaler was selling double counterweighted holders with two weights on the end of an upside-down V-shaped wire. The makers used small lead weights cast in molds shaped like little pine cones, acorns, stars, birds, and cherubs.

Unfortunately, counterweighted candleholders had one inherent flaw. The counterweights, by necessity, doubled the weight of the candle alone; thus they could not be used on any small branch, or anyplace they could slip off as trees dried out and limbs began to droop. A counterweighted candleholder could slide off a branch and start a fire.

In 1879, New Yorker Frederick Arzt invented a spring-clip candleholder. Even though American and German manufacturers, as well as Arzt himself, continued for years to try to improve on his original idea, the clip-on Christmas tree candleholder quickly became the public's favorite. When it came to holding a candle perfectly straight, a clip-on couldn't hold a candle to a counterweight, but it was safer.

Clip-ons remained popular until candles finally went out of fashion in this country during the 1920s. They were invariably made from tin, and the clip was frequently decorated in relief with little birds, pine cones, or a tiny hand, and painted in bright colors. Most continued to be imported from Germany, where a luxury model—a brilliant lithographed tin butterfly—was developed early in the century.

There was a practical reason behind the aesthetically pleasing spiral-shaped candles used on Victorian Christmas trees. Their shape was intended to prevent dripping wax, a real problem with old-fashioned tallow candles. Though only partially successful, the idea was nonetheless a good one. Because of its shape this type of candle was known as a "cable" candle, and it was made in many colors, including the traditional red, white, and green. In 1889 delicate pink and pale blue tapers were reported to be fashionable.

In New York and other big cities, many of these molded tallow candles were not supplied by large manufacturers, but were made by Italian immigrants who labored late into the night in tenement kitchens each November and December. As Christmas approached, their homemade candles were often sold on the streets by poor children and peddlers.

The danger of fire from candles was of course always present, even more so in America, where many houses were constructed entirely of wood. (In Germany electric tree lights have never replaced the beautiful burning candle.) There seem to have been fewer Christmas tree fires than might be expected, but there is no denying the impact of their tragedy. When a Christmas tree caught fire, the best of times suddenly turned into the worst.

A search through old newspapers turns up infinitely more Christmas-time fires caused by exploding oil lamps, chimney fires, and curtains blown against gas jets than by candles on trees. Trees were usually fresher and greener in those days and had remained out in the cold until late Christmas Eve, since children were taught to believe Santa Claus brought the trees. They knew that their parents stored the ornaments for Santa in their attic and brought them down for him the night before Christmas, but they believed that Santa himself decorated the tree and put the candles on it.

Many trees were literally covered with candles; a contemporary magazine recommended four hundred candles for a twelve-foot tree. Each candle had to be placed ever so carefully so there was nothing above it. Lighting candles was adults' work, as children watched and usually received a safety lecture at the same time.

A miniature oil lamp for the Christmas tree was patented by John Barth in 1887.

After Christmas, trees did not dry out quickly because houses were not as well heated or well insulated as they are today. Each night the room in which the tree stood became a natural ice box. But with each passing year there were more Christmas trees, and more fires. Newspapers printed news of the tragedies even though they may have occurred halfway across the country.

In 1885 a candle-lit tree caught fire during a Christmas Eve festivity in a Chicago hospital. High atop a giant twenty-five-foot tree, heavily laden with presents, a candle suddenly spluttered, leaned over, and touched the tree. Flames leaped up, and in less than half a minute the entire tree was a howling mass of flame. Five hundred and eighty-five patients and their friends were lucky enough to escape alive from the fire and the ensuing panic, but many persons were trampled upon and badly bruised.

Throughout the 1880s and 1890s newspaper accounts of tree fires in the houses and apartments of Americans with names like McCabe and Higgins show that, despite the dangers, people of non-German ancestry had begun to adopt the Christmas tree.

People read the following sad account of a Christmas fatality in 1897:

MATAWAN, N.J., Dec. 25.—Until this evening Christmas was a joyous one in the home of Robert Morris, a colored man, at the corner of Broad and Atlantic Streets, Keyport. Now there is gloom, brought on by the burning to death of one of the members of the family.

Shortly before 5 o'clock this evening Mrs. Morris decided to light the candles of the Christmas tree, which stood in the front room. Frank Morris, her six-year-old son, was close beside her as she with the matches first touched one candle and then another. Frank became over-anxious, and seizing hold of a branch of the Christmas tree to see whether one of the candles was lighting, he upset the tree. In an instant the whole tree was on fire, as well as the ornaments which adorned it. The tree in falling set fire to the house, and also to the clothing of Frank. He screamed, but at first it was thought he was shrieking on account of the fire. When it was discovered that Frank's clothing was ablaze, an attempt was made to put out the fire on him. It was too late, however. He was carried out of the house but had been frightfully burned from head to foot and died in a few minutes. The house, a little frame structure, was also burned down, causing a loss of about $500. Coroner Theodore Anderson went to Keyport, saw the body of the burned youngster, and granted a permit for burial.

Fires claimed the trees of the rich as well as the poor. In 1904 a blaze stopped a party and destroyed a Bridgeport, Connecticut, mansion on the day after Christmas. The press reported:

The handsome residence of Col. and Mrs. Tracey B. Warren in Seaview Avenue, facing Long Island Sound, was burned today, a candle which was part of the decoration of a Christmas tree starting the blaze. Col. and Mrs. Warren were entertaining a party of children at the time.

All the persons in the house got out safely, but in her anxiety for the children, Mrs. Warren neglected some valuable jewels. The contents of the house were consumed. The loss is estimated at $12,000, partly insured.

Even in the first years of the twentieth century, an old-fashioned custom still prevailing among a large number of German-American families added to the danger of tree fires by prolonging the time that a tree stood inside the home before it was lighted. The tree would arrive secretly, while the children were out of the house, sometimes a week or more before Christmas. Nonetheless, the watchful children were alerted to the tree's presence by suddenly locked parlor doors and a stuffed keyhole. An exciting aura of mystery surrounded the well-secured chamber into which Father, or sometimes Father and Mother both, would retire in the evenings to decorate the tree with all manner of candies, mottoes, cookies, and other ornaments. These would be interspersed with colored candles, which would be lighted for the first time just before the parlor doors were thrown wide open on Christmas Eve.

Throughout the latter part of the nineteenth century and during the beginning of this one, candle-lit trees were an integral part of public Christmas celebrations, occasionally with heartbreaking results. In 1900 a little girl was burned to death in a New York City school as a result of her snow fairy costume, made of a light flimsy material, catching fire as she helped to distribute gifts from the tree. The Board of Education, appalled by the occurrence, issued an order that never again should a lighted candle be used in connection with Christmas tree entertainments.

In both New York and Chicago young nurses were burned to death before the eyes of horrified children, as a result of backing into the lighted Christmas trees at hospital children's-ward parties.

Out of New York State, Detroit, Michigan, and Washington, D.C., came stories about the burning of Santa Clauses who leaned over to pick up a present and brushed a tree candle with their flammable cotton beards.

Surprisingly, there was almost no editorial outcry against Christmas tree candles in the newspapers and magazines of the day. A few did suggest that one or two buckets of water should be placed near any Christmas tree on which tapers would be lighted, as well as a tin cup or two in which to throw water. Some writers advised that a family appoint one member to be the fire warden, whose job it was to watch the tree at all times when the candles were lighted, armed with a big wet sponge on the end of a long cane. This advice was followed by many, including Franklin D. Roosevelt, who throughout the 1920s insisted on candles on his fourteen-foot trees at Hyde Park, New York.

By the early 1900s many people had become sufficiently frightened by tree-fire stories to forgo the old pleasure of a candle-lit tree. Others couldn't give it up, even though they worried every time they

Two examples of spring-
clip candleholders.

lit the candles. For instance, in 1905 an Ohio family that had always
had candles on its trees changed its usual tradition. Unable to give
up candles entirely, it decided to limit the tree lighting to five minutes
at 11 o'clock on Christmas morning. All morning the tension built
toward that brief enchanted period. After breakfast the children had
to make their beds, then do one more chore and one more chore, until
at last it was time. As they gathered around the candle-covered tree,
which Grandfather always lit, Grandmother, Mother, Father, and each
of the children stood around the tree with a pan or bucket filled with
water in case disaster struck. Grandfather lit the candles for five
minutes of oohing and aahing, and then he carefully blew them out
until next year.

Insurance companies caused many people to give up the candle-lit tree. In 1908 a number of the underwriters began a concerted campaign to kill the candle. They publicly disclaimed their liability in Christmas tree fires, pointing out that all insurance policies had always carried a clause that stated: "This policy is invalidated if the holder takes knowing risks." It is probably to the credit of insurance companies that they made good for as many Christmas fires as they did.

Over the years many attempts were made to find safer ways of lighting a tree, the most extreme version being an iron tree made by an English firm. It was lit by gas and advertised as the "Improved German Christmas Tree." In 1859, at St. James Lutheran Church in New York City, an evergreen was lighted by nearly two hundred gas jets that had been carefully built into it. In the years that followed other trees were similarly lighted.

Early glass factories in this country made a product known as "Christmas lights." During the Victorian era these tumblerlike glasses were suspended from the branches of many fashionable trees, lighted by a wick attached to a piece of wood or cork that floated in oil atop water. The lights came in clear or colored glass, in several patterns including hob nails, diamond cut, and the "thousand eye" pattern, a combination of round and diamond facets cleverly designed to reflect ten tiny points of flickering light in each of its one hundred "eyes."

When Jenny Lind visited Charleston, South Carolina, in 1850, touring under the auspices of P. T. Barnum, the ladies of the city placed Christmas lights on a tree outside her window on Christmas Eve.

This type of light was not unique to Yuletide illumination. The same lights were sometimes used for garden fetes, church functions, and patriotic celebrations. In colonial days, the American glassmaker "Baron" Stiegel is believed to have handblown a light of this sort, now in the Metropolitan Museum of Art in New York, but not until inexpensive pressed-glass versions came in did these lights become really popular on Christmas trees. Their only disadvantage on a tree was their weight, which was considerable.

In the late 1870s tiny, eight-sided tin lanterns with windows of isinglass began to appear on American trees. They held a small candle the size of a birthday-cake candle, which shone through thin windows that were often colored amber, red, green, or blue. These lanterns not only provided a slight advantage in terms of safety, but they also kept wax from falling on the carpet.

In 1887 John Barth of Louisville, Kentucky, patented a miniature oil lamp with a glass protective globe. It was designed to take the place of candles, particularly on Christmas trees in churches and schools. Barth's Christmas-Tree Lamp was featured in *Scientific American* that year, but because his invention appeared four years after the first electrically lighted Christmas tree, it has since disappeared almost without a trace.

The frustrating and dangerous problem of the Christmas tree candle that would not stand perfectly upright, no matter how carefully the tree trimmer tried to place it on a bough, continued to challenge the ingenuity of candleholder manufacturers. By 1910 there were several new types of candleholders, each one designed to be tied around the end of an evergreen branch. In one example, the candleholder was attached to the end of a coil of soft wire, which could be easily attached and bent to the desired upright position. Another candleholder was attached to the end of a six-inch strip of tin, which was wrapped several times around the bough before the candle was inserted and adjusted.

By 1920 the Germans had applied more sophisticated technology to the old classic, the clip-on candleholder. Greater safety was achieved with the simple addition of an adjustable ball and socket joint that could be rotated to the desired position. The little device worked amazingly well, but it arrived too late to compete with the newer and safer miracle of electricity.

With electricity it was possible to improve on the safety of an open candle on a Christmas tree, but never on its beauty. Despite the fear of fire, many families used candles for years after tree lights were available.

At the turn of this century the George W. Vanderbilts switched to the newly fashionable electric tree lights, having more than five hundred electric bulbs wired onto the big thirty-foot tree in the banquet hall at their estate in Asheville, North Carolina. The colorful modern effect must have disappointed at least some of the family members, because in 1905 they returned for one last time to a candle-lit Christmas tree.

A chandelier-style counterweighted candle- holder; the pendants were stamped from tin.

VII
THE CANDLES
FADE OUT,
TREE LIGHTS COME ON

n New Year's Eve, 1879, three thousand people flooded into the little town of Menlo Park, New Jersey, to see Thomas Alva Edison demonstrate for the first time in public the light bulb he had invented on October 21 of that year. His laboratory, the streets of Menlo Park, and some of its houses were illuminated by electric lights.

Just three years later the world's first electrically lighted Christmas tree was decorated in the New York City home of Edward Johnson, a colleague of Edison's at the newly formed Edison Electric Company. He lived in the first square mile of the first city in the world to have electricity. The event was not reported in the New York papers of the day but it was seen and recorded by a young reporter named Croffut for the *Detroit Post and Tribune*. Croffut's story began:

Last evening I walked over beyond Fifth Avenue and called at the residence of Edward H. Johnson, vice-president of Edison's electric

The first electric Christmas tree lights on Edward Johnson's tree, New York City, 1882.

company. There, at the rear of the beautiful parlors, was a large Christmas tree presenting a most picturesque and uncanny aspect. It was brilliantly lighted with many colored globes about as large as an English walnut and was turning some six times a minute on a little pine box. There were 80 lights in all encased in these dainty glass eggs, and about equally divided between white, red and blue. As the tree turned, the colors alternated, all the lamps going out and being relit at every revolution. The rest was a continuous twinkling of dancing colors, red, white, blue, white, red, blue—all evening.

I need not tell you that the scintillating evergreen was a pretty sight—one can hardly imagine anything prettier. The ceiling was crossed obliquely with two wires on which hung 28 more of the tiny lights; and all the lights and the fantastic tree itself with its starry fruit were kept going by the slight electric current brought from the main office on a filmy wire. The tree was kept revolving by a little hidden crank below the floor which was turned by electricity. It was a superb exhibition.

It is hard to imagine today the scope of Edison's achievements in the few short years between 1877, when he first began his incandescent light experiments, and the Christmas of 1882, when someone in his laboratory hand-blew the bulbs and hand-wired the lights on Edward Johnson's Christmas tree. Edison had invented not only the light bulb, but also the component parts of a central electric-generating station, without which widespread use of his electric lights would not have been practical. He also developed a metering system, which made possible from the beginning the selling of electricity according to exact units of use.

Within a few years Edison's electric company expanded to include the manufacture of light bulbs, and soon he was making miniature bulbs for decorative purposes, like electric candles and chandeliers, in a wholly electrified factory at Harrison, New Jersey.

Immediately the novel idea of electric lights on the Christmas tree became the rage among the wealthy, who either lived in an area just electrified or, like banking baron J. P. Morgan, could afford to put in their own generator. Once they had electricity, they had to find someone who knew how to wire a number of individual miniature lights and sockets on the tree. Christmas tree parties to show off the expensive, electrically lighted trees became exciting social events for children of high society.

In 1895 President Cleveland added electric lights to his tree in the White House. Both his tree and his daughter's eyes were said to have sparkled with the electrical effects. Conspicuous among the other ornaments on their electric tree were gold angels with wide-spreading wings, gold and silver sleds, toys of every description, and tinsel.

At a New York City hospital some wealthy benefactor paid to have a tree wired each Christmas, perhaps as a result of reading about the terrifying tree fire and the panic caused by a falling candle at a Chicago hospital in 1885. The following account appeared in *The New York Times* on December 25, 1891:

The children's ward of the New York Hospital was aglow last night with hundreds of lights that shone on a big Christmas tree in the middle of the room. Around it were gathered all the children of the ward, some propped up with pillows and others running about on the floor, all clad in warm red jackets and all alike beaming with pleasure. With them were fifty nurses in dainty blue and white gowns and caps. There was a present for everyone, nurses and children alike, and the big tree fairly groaned with its weight of good things. The tree itself was a sight to see. It was so arranged as to revolve slowly, and as it moved, electric lights shone from each of its boughs. The children, many of whom had never seen anything half so fine, shouted with delight.

By 1894 the *Times* felt compelled to attack editorially the new notion that one had to have electric lights in order to have a wonderful Christmas tree, for the costs were very high—probably the equivalent of one to two thousand dollars today.

The little children of the rich have grown critical with over-abundance, and nothing short of an electric tree, with fairy effects produced by that wizard bower, satisfies them. It is easy to spend $100 on the electricity alone if it is brought into the house for this single service, and even if the residence is wire-strung the tree bulbs will cost a dollar each to attach. As a big tree takes anywhere from thirty to fifty to be sufficiently dazzling, the least expensive arrangement is by no means cheap.

In 1890 General Electric bought Edison's rights and his light-bulb factory. In 1901, in an attempt to popularize lights on Christmas trees, GE put out a booklet extolling their virtues. A small advertisement offering it ran in both the *Ladies' Home Journal* and *Scientific American*. According to the booklet:

Miniature incandescent lamps are perfectly adapted to Christmas tree lighting. The element of danger ever present with candles is entirely removed, as well as the inconvenience of grease, smoke, and dirt. The lamps are all lighted at once by the turning of a switch, will burn as long as desired without attention, and can be readily extinguished. Miniature lamps can be placed in locations where candles could not be used, and much greater freedom is thus allowed in Christmas tree decoration with electric lamps. Lamps of various sizes can be adapted for different sizes of trees and the most charming effects produced by the use of lamps of different colors.

Even though GE manufactured light bulbs, strings of lights as we know them today were not yet being produced. Individual bulbs could be bought outright or leased from the company.

The booklet also contained diagrams to show the "wireman," the electrician of that decade, how to wire the tree. A single series was made up of thirty-two tiny bulbs, thirty-two porcelain sockets, rubber-coated wire, and a larger screw socket to fit into the power outlet (usually the ceiling chandelier). The wireman cut thirty-two short lengths of wire and stripped each end so that it could be connected to the socket with a brass screw. This process continued from socket to socket until a complete strand of lights had been assembled.

Before the advent of ready-made strings of lights, the idea of electric lights for Christmas trees was totally impractical for the average family. Hand-wiring a tree required electrical skills and a disproportionate amount of time.

The Ever-Ready Company of New York, seeing the need, began manufacturing and marketing strings of lights in 1903, calling them "festoons" or "outfits." General Electric sold these strings of twenty-eight sockets with GE bulbs for twelve dollars, an average man's weekly wages.

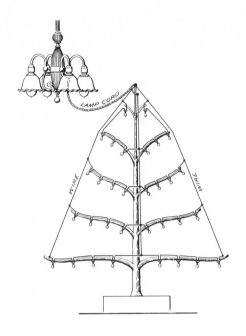

This diagram from a 1901 booklet published by General Electric shows how individual light bulbs could be wired together and then wired into an electric fixture, in the days before Christmas tree lights came in strings.

By 1907, Ever-Ready was putting out a standard series-wired set with eight light sockets. By wiring these sets together, a set of sixteen, twenty-four, or thirty-two lights could be made.

Louis Szel, a pioneer in the early lighting business, has described the manner in which Ever-Ready strings were made in 1907 and for years thereafter:

The wire was taken from reels mounted at the end of long worktables. A man took the end of the wire and ran to the other end of the bench where he began looping the wire around a series of eight pairs of steel pegs. Each of the eight loops were then tied in a slip knot. Each loop was then cut, the ends of the wires stripped by hand and the sockets were pushed over the ends of the wires. The wires were then soldered with table-mounted soldering irons that moved up and down by a foot pedal to the brass screw shells. One wire was soldered to the center of the brass shell at the base and the other to the side of the screw shell. Then the shells were cemented into their little green porcelain sockets.

The young men who did the job of looping the wire were paid on a piece work basis and actually ran or most of the time slid for greater speed over the wooden factory floors, so that the floor became as slick and slippery as an ice skating rink. The workers' hands became terribly calloused and some of them had hard skin ridges on their hands up to half an inch deep from pulling the rough, cotton covered wire and making knots all day.

However, Ever-Ready did not have a patent on the wiring system, since it was based only on common knowledge that any "wirer" or electrician had, and many other smaller companies began manufacturing these strings of lights.

Despite all these advances, however, the average American of 1907 was still unaware of electric Christmas tree lights. One such man was Ralph Morris, a telephone man who lived in Matapan, Massachusetts. On Christmas night in 1907 his tree was lighted by two large standing candles. A near tragedy occurred when his four-year-old son Leavitt, crawling around the base of the tree, knocked over one of the candles and singed his hair.

Ralph Morris, who did not know that General Electric was manufacturing electric tree lights, devised his own electric lights for the following Christmas, using the clear bulbs from the inside of a telephone switchboard. He soldered them to a long wire and wrapped colored crepe paper around them with rubber bands. That Christmas night, with four generations of his family assembled around his tree, he asked his grandmother to pull an electric switch. Suddenly the tree and the darkened room was illuminated.

For the rest of his life, and throughout much of his son's, the Morris family sincerely believed Ralph Morris had invented Christmas tree lights in 1908. In 1952 Leavitt Morris recalled the magic of that electric tree lighting in an article for the *Christian Science Monitor*. His article revealed that although his father never knew it, Christmas tree lights had been invented twenty-five years earlier.

As little companies went into, and often just as quickly out of, the tree-lighting business, a new concern rose in the public's mind. The danger might be less than burning candles, but faulty strings of lights were causing a new wave of tree fires. Underwriters' Laboratories tested and first established safety requirements for Christmas tree lights in 1921. The UL seal on a box quickly became important in merchandising and has been almost a prerequisite for three generations.

Early in this century, even though most people in rural parts of this country did not have electricity, they could still have a modern, electrically lighted Christmas tree. The early sets of lights could be wired to several wet- or dry-celled batteries.

Before the end of World War I General Electric replaced Edison's carbon filament with longer-lasting tungsten filaments and sold miniature "Mazda" lamps for Christmas trees. The trade name Mazda had been used on GE's regular full-sized light bulbs since 1910, as a symbol of good service, representing the best light bulbs modern science could produce. Other companies were able to buy rights to the use of the Mazda technology and trademark, including Westinghouse, which printed "Westinghouse-Mazda" on their own light bulbs.

The next important development came in 1923 with the introduction of the "Tachon" connector, invented by Lester Haft. It replaced the little emerald-green porcelain junction boxes that had been the usual means of wiring several series-wired light sets into one larger unit. The original Haft connector, which was produced before blade-type plugs, was a screw plug and socket. The socket had a screw-in cover attached by a short string, a safety device to prevent people from leaving an open socket in the last set connected.

This simple device gave Haft's employer, the C. D. Wood Electric Company, a tremendous competitive advantage. They immediately licensed fourteen other companies that made light strings to manufacture the Tachon device, and collected a royalty of three cents for each one manufactured. In 1925 the Tachon connector became the basis for the fifteen companies to form a trade association, and in 1927 they all merged into one giant company, NOMA (National Outfit Manufacturers Association), which is still in business. NOMA, together with its light-bulb suppliers, General Electric and Westinghouse, has dominated the Christmas light business in America ever since.

Many years later the patent for the helpful little Tachon connector, or as it would eventually become known, the "tri-plug," was withdrawn. When challenged by NOMA's competitors, the courts ruled that it was based on the skill of any good electrician and therefore should never have been considered a patentable invention.

The next great leap forward in light strings came from GE in 1927. Anyone who has ever gingerly crawled around through a fully decorated Christmas tree in search of the one burned-out bulb that put off all the rest of the lights can appreciate what GE did when they switched from the old "series" wired set to "parallel" wiring.

In "series" wiring used for tree lights, the normal 120-volt current is divided into eight, lighting eight small 15-volt bulbs. If one bulb burned out, the broken filament interrupted the flow of current and all the other lights in that set went off.

However, in "parallel" wiring, the type used for general household lighting by the 1920s, each light bulb was in direct contact with 120 volts. To use the same system for Christmas tree lighting, a special small bulb, which would not get too hot for use on a tree, had to be developed. The solution was a coiled filament wire that had to be less than one-thousandth of an inch in diameter and nearly sixteen inches long. In 1927 General Electric finally found a way to produce such a filament, by coiling hair-thin wire around a thicker wire called a "mandrel." When a mandrel many feet long had been completely wrapped, the coils were cut to one-inch lengths and the mandrel in the middle was chemically dissolved away.

Since new parallel sets had to be bought in order to use GE's ingenious new bulbs, most people continued to use their old series sets until long after World War II, and they can still be purchased today. They are cheaper, because they use only half as much wire.

Other attempts have been made to solve the old series problem. In 1949 the Japanese introduced "shunting" type bulbs, with a fine wire in the base. When the filament blew out, the current fused this thin shunt to the lead-in wires, completing the circuit to the other lights. One bulb was out but the other seven continued to burn. However, the same voltage, when spread among fewer lights, made those bulbs burn out faster.

At about the same time Westinghouse came out with an interesting solution to the same problem, combining the shunting principle with neon gas. When the filament burned out, the "Detecto" bulb went dark but the base continued to glow, which made it easier to spot and replace.

While these technological improvements were being made the shape of the bulb itself was also undergoing change. Edison's and General Electric's original tree bulbs were miniature editions of the

Three Austrian figurative light bulbs.

household light bulb of the day. They had been designed as night lights for a larger market, but the companies soon discovered a secondary market in Christmas trees. These bulbs were the classic light-bulb shape, like an upside-down pear, about one inch wide at the widest point and one and a half inches high, including the screw base. The bulbs came to a sharp point at the top, where the air was exhausted and the molten glass was sealed.

In about 1910 General Electric changed its miniature bulbs to a ball shape, one inch in diameter and perfectly round except for the exhaust tip on top. Color was added by dipping the bulbs into a transparent lacquer. But in the early 1920s General Electric experimented with the shape of its basic-series bulb and came up with a corrugated cone shape. It quickly sold so much better than the ball-shaped bulb that GE dropped the old shape completely. By the time it was ready to market the new bulb in parallel-wired "multiple" light sets, the bulb was a fuller noncorrugated version of the cone shape. By this time the bulbs were colored by spraying rather than by dipping.

Aside from the technical advances made in electric lights, many decorative innovations were made. During the Christmas season of 1909 figurative miniature light bulbs became available. The first were hand-made and hand-painted in Austria by the Kremenetzky Electric Company of Vienna. They were shaped and colored to look like glass fruits, flowers, birds, and animals. The fruits included an apple, an orange, a peach, a pear, and a strawberry; the flowers were lilies, roses, and thistles; and there were also a canary, clown, dog, owl, snowman, and most important, a Santa Claus figure. Figurative lights were later made in Germany, Japan, and the United States, but until the 1930s none compared with the delicacy of the glass and the painting on the original Viennese product.

The early figurative bulbs made by General Electric were also hand-made and hand-painted, but by 1919 the General Electric plant in Cleveland, Ohio, was manufacturing machine-blown lights. They were produced in a great many shapes, including animals, stars, tulips, and a Santa Claus.

With the beginning of World War I, direct importation of Austrian tree lights stopped, although they continued to trickle in through Italy. America's entry into the war in 1917 put an end to this arrangement.

At about the same time, the importer Louis Szel sailed to Japan looking for a source of figure lights. He spent a year laying the foundation for the Japanese Christmas tree light industry, the basis for which was a small colony of glass makers in and around Tokyo. Szel dealt with a number of "lamp makers," who subcontracted to even smaller home workshops for glassblowing, setting of the filaments, heat sealing, basing, exhausting, and finally the spraying and hand-painting of the fancy figurative light bulbs.

The early glassblowing methods of the Japanese were extremely primitive and the thickness of the glass was cruder than in the finely blown Austrian product. Austrian glass was transparent before painting, while most Japanese glass was translucent white milk glass.

The first designs created by the Japanese mold makers were poor imitations of the handblown Austrian bulbs and German glass ornaments. Over the years, however, with the development of bulbs in the form of cartoon characters such as Popeye, Little Orphan Annie, Andy and Min Gump, and Dick Tracy, an indefinable Oriental flavor crept into the Japanese mold and painting. Even Santa Claus bore a distinct resemblance to Buddha. Although quality was poor at first and the life of the bulbs was short, no European lamps were available because of the war, and so the Japanese products were readily accepted by the American public.

In the home workshops much of the blowing was done by youngsters, mostly boys from eight to fourteen years old and sometimes younger. One child would squat on the floor holding the hinged metal mold ajar while a second youngster would dangle the red-hot end of a glass tube between the two halves. When the mold was snapped closed, the blower would blow hard enough to force the glass to expand to the walls of the mold.

Small brick furnaces were set up in the open just outside the workshop to lessen the fire hazard. The little glassblower would heat the end of his glass tube in the fire, then turn around and complete the molding process beneath an overhanging roof, so that the rain could not disrupt his work, winter or summer.

The glass used by the Japanese had a very high lead content, and blowing into the red-hot tubes for twelve to fourteen hours a day exposed the children's lungs to excessive amounts of lead. In many cases they became tubercular and died. There were no child-labor laws in Japan in those days, and millions of children worked at equally difficult and dangerous trades.

The father of the house would usually see to the fire in the furnace and supervise the work. While his own children were sometimes part of the work crew, in many cases they came from other families poorer than his. The children who blew the glass received about fifty sen per day (twenty-five cents at the exchange rate of that time), and perhaps some hot tea several times during the day and dried fish with rice for lunch.

There was endless toil in each phase of the production of a single light bulb. The last step was the painting—hand painting in the case of the figurative bulbs. The painters applied large areas of color with an airbrush, also operated by mouth and lung. Eyes, nostrils, mouths, buttons, and other details were quickly applied with tiny brushes.

123

Japanese milk-glass light bulbs.

During the 1930s many of America's favorite comic characters appeared
on the Christmas tree in figurative light bulbs made in Japan.

The paint was the reason Japanese bulbs were made from milk glass. In 1917 the first ones produced were copies of the clear Austrian bulbs, but the Japanese were unable to copy the paint used by the Viennese craftsmen. Their first efforts cracked and chipped and stuck to the rice-paper tissue they were shipped in. When the bulbs were lighted, the cracks showed clearly and exposed the filament inside the bulb. To overcome this problem, in 1918 they began to blow their bulbs from tubes of milk glass. Later, even though their paint improved, the Japanese continued to use milk glass.

The lamp maker would pack the bulbs in rough brown cardboard boxes, twenty-five, fifty, or one hundred bulbs to a box. Shipping the product involved some hard labor. Transport to the port of Yokohama was by rail, but from the lamp maker's house to the railroad, and then to the docks in Yokohama, men and women had to pull the boxes on big two-wheeled handcarts. The carts were eight to ten feet long and attached to each was a heavy rope with a leather strap into which the human "horse" put his shoulder. Coolies often had to pull these heavily loaded carts long distances up steep hills. In the summer when a man's shirt was off, one could see a two- to three-inch indentation in his shoulder from the strap.

The Japanese Christmas-lamp industry was developed to a much higher level of efficiency in the late 1920s and 1930s as a number of old lamp makers became small manufacturers with specially built plants. The Japanese bought machines for exhausting, paint spraying, and automatic filament setting from a company in New Jersey, and produced countless millions of little light bulbs between 1917 and 1941. Until the 1950s, however, they made no strings of Christmas tree lights for the American market.

The once-popular Japanese figurative lights were victims of World War II. When occupied Japan went back into the business of supplying Christmas bulbs after the war, America moved temporarily toward the oversimplified modernity of colored floodlights flashed on aluminum trees. Figurative bulbs were out of fashion and were quickly dropped by retailers.

Nowadays many people who still have the old prewar figurative lights will not give them up even when they burn out and the strings have to be abandoned. They hang the unlighted Santa Claus, the little comic-strip figures, the cowboy and the Indian, the cat and the fiddle on their tree with their other ornaments.

Beginning in 1936, under a license from Walt Disney Productions, NOMA Lites produced something entirely new in Christmas tree lights: strings of standard-series bulbs dressed up with little brightly colored plastic "lamp shades." Each little shade was decorated with a decal of a Disney character. Thus Mickey Mouse, Donald Duck, Pluto, and Snow White made their appearance on American Christmas trees.

The biggest Christmas light "bubble" of the postwar years began with an accountant who was also a basement inventor and textbook chemist. In the late 1930s Carl Otis, an accountant for Montgomery Ward, got the idea for the bubble light. It was based on methaline chloride, a liquid that will "boil" merrily at a relatively low temperature in a properly exhausted vial. His idea was to combine a bubbling vial of colored methaline chloride with the heat and light of a Christmas tree bulb. Otis was invited to join NOMA in order to develop his idea, but the war delayed production of the invention. "Bubble-Lites" were finally launched in 1945 with all the fanfare of a press conference, including a pretty model. Sales were average at first, but by the middle 1950s the new lights caught the public's fancy. Sales were spectacular for a few years, then the sales curve went down like a roller coaster.

Like those other phenomena of the 1950s, the hula hoop and the twist, the spectacular success of bubble lights contributed to their failure. At first they were a novelty and a conversation piece, but once everyone had the same novelty, it lost its value. Just as the initial attraction was wearing thin, however, a new competitor entered the market place—midget light sets—and suddenly everything went wrong for the bubble light. As soon as sales began to skid, NOMA had trouble getting independent wholesalers and retailers to stock replacement bulbs, and in the 1960s F. W. Woolworth was the only major retailer that continued to sell bubble lights.

In the 1970s Americans began to experience a wave of nostalgia for the 1950s. Out of the attic came a few old "BubbleLite" sets that still worked. A new generation of children had never seen anything like the brightly colored bubbling lights, and suddenly adults found they were once again a conversation piece. In 1972 the several companies that still made them experienced a surprising new demand for these bubbling ghosts of Christmases past.

Their successors on American Christmas trees began arriving in this country from Italy, Holland, Switzerland, Germany, and Japan. Midget light sets with miniature bulbs about three-quarters-inch long and less than one-quarter-inch wide took over the market. The little bulbs created an entirely new effect on the Christmas tree. With up to forty-eight white lights of low candlepower on the same string, they could be clustered close together so that they reminded people of stars in the night sky.

From the beginning the midget lights were wired in series, but if one burned out, there were even more little bulbs to check than with the older lights. This early drawback was soon solved by the application of a shunt circuit-completing device, and next came the push-in bulb and socket.

Christmas tree lights that flashed on and off had been available since the 1930s, but most people found them too interruptive for their living rooms. Flashing midget lights were a different story. Marketed as midget twinkle lights, they became the biggest sellers in the history of tree lights.

Since novelty is the key to increased sales in the Christmas light business, each year brings new variations from the makers of midget lights. There have been tiny lighted plastic snowmen and Santas, stockings and candy canes, little houses that form a lighted miniature village on the Christmas tree, and even a set of midget lights with a tiny stable and figures of the Holy Family. By the Christmas of 1974 retailers were selling sets of midget bubble lights that were only one-quarter the size of the original bubbling candles.

In all their continuously changing forms, electric tree lights are the uniquely American contribution to the Christmas tree.

Fragile old Christmas tree decorations made from paper-thin glass. The cross-section of ornaments on the preceding three and the following two pages are examples of the craft originated and perfected by glassblowers in the German village of Lauscha. Detailed figurative designs were blown in molds like the one for the snowman above.

Wax figures and soft tin objects in geometric designs were among the oldest Christmas tree ornaments. Like these, the cotton-batting ornaments (right) were the product of German cottage labor.

A representative selection of embossed cardboard ornaments made in Dresden between the 1800s and 1910. Most of this type of ornament were either silver or gold, but some were painstakingly hand-painted in a realistic manner.

Many cardboard ornaments, like the musical instruments and the collection of drums, the house, and the birdcage, were little candy boxes in disguise. Each of the little shoes on these pages hung from a silk bag that could conceal a tiny gift.

Two glass oil-burning "Christmas lights" and a tiny candle-burning lantern like those that lighted many turn-of-the-century trees. Below is a variety of clip-on and counterweighted holders.

A typical treetop electric star of the 1930s.

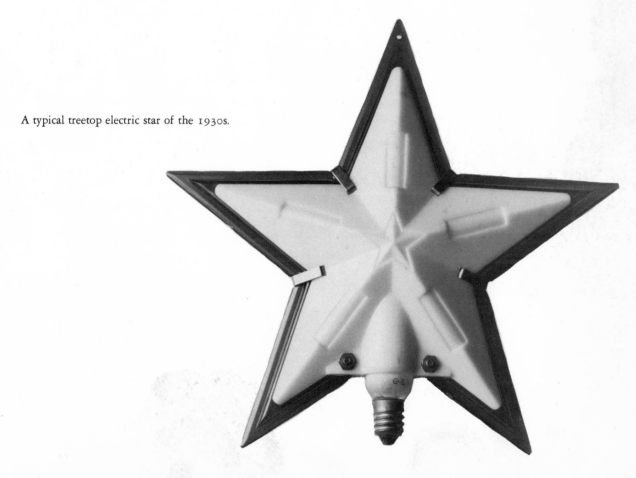

OPPOSITE: Figurative light bulbs for the Christmas
tree made in the 1920s and 1930s.

A Christmas Eve mishap, illustrated in an 1865 woodcut.

VIII
THE MAGIC WORLD
UNDER THE
CHRISTMAS TREE

n the nineteenth century it was no small feat to persuade a large evergreen to stand upright in a parlor. Many trees were literally replanted in large containers filled with dirt and rocks. In January 1856 the *Guardian* described the planting of a tree in a wooden box covered with paper; the surface of the dirt was covered with moss, which again was covered with little heaps of almonds, figs, raisins, and all kinds of nuts. Here and there were placed an orange, a coconut, and apples to make it look even richer.

Old illustrations of the smaller German trees invariably show the trunk secured to a flat board or a low stool or nailed to crosslike wooden feet. These were adequate to hold up a small German table tree, but for a long time there was a need, in this country, for ways in which to re-erect the unwieldy evergreen.

147

A family around the Christmas tree, listening to the musical tree stand, 1890.

In Washington, D.C., on October 10, 1876, Hermann Albrecht and Abram C. Mott, Philadelphians who had worked together on the problem, were granted the first and second United States patents ever given for Christmas tree stands. While somewhat different in appearance, each looked like a three-legged iron flag stand, a secondary use both men mentioned in their applications. Within three years Albrecht had another idea and in 1880 he received a patent for an improved design; his new holder gripped the tree's trunk firmly by means of a ring around a cylinderlike socket, which would, when screwed upward, force three cleats against the trunk. All these tree stands were designed to be screwed to the floor or to some larger base for greater stability.

In 1877 a man from Stuttgart, Johannes C. Eckardt, applied for an American patent for a revolving musical tree stand. The user would place the tree's trunk in an iron socket case in the shape of a pine cone, and when the spring mechanism was wound up, the tree would rotate slowly while a small music box concealed in its circular base played a Christmas tune. Eckardt, like Albrecht, couldn't stop tinkering with his idea and he was subsequently granted three more patents for mechanical improvements to the original design, which remained popular for forty years.

Throughout the 1880s and 1890s Americans with German names such as Merk, Schoenthaler, Westphal, and Langenbach, gave thought to the tree stand and received patents for their efforts. Literally and figuratively, the high-water mark in flag-stand-type tree stands was achieved in 1899 when Alfred Wagner of St. Louis received a patent for a stand that was rotated by an electric motor; it was also the first Christmas tree stand designed with a cup to hold water for the tree.

Despite the general availability of iron tree stands in the 1890s, they were not cheap and most home trees even in the early years of this century were still erected with inexpensive homemade methods. Tree sellers, recognizing that a tree that would stand alone had a greatly increased value to a prospective purchaser, kept legions of small boys employed mounting trees upright with crude tripod arrangements made by tying or nailing pieces of wood to the base.

By 1900 magazines suggested the use of coal in a bucket for the purpose. Coal was readily available in most households and could be tightly packed around the tree's trunk; water could also be added to help keep the tree fresh for a longer period of time. Since even a bucket filled with coal and water provided none-too-heavy a base for a ten-foot tree, everything from bricks to rocks was added on top to assure the tree would stay upright. It was not uncommon for the household's flatirons to be lined up around the trunk. The big tin tree stand with the built-in pan for water did not become a familiar accessory to the Christmas tree until after 1914.

In addition to the tree stand there developed another charming custom, which had originally been practiced by the same Pennsylvania Germans who gave America the Christmas tree. Around the base of their tree a *Putz* or Christmas tree yard was constructed. The term was derived from the German verb *putzen,* which means to decorate. No two were alike but originally they all represented the stable scene with the Child and Mary and Joseph. A great deal of time and effort was devoted to their production, especially among the German-speaking Moravians who settled in the vicinity of Bethlehem, Pennsylvania, where *Putz* building is still a revered tradition.

From colonial days onward the Moravians made more of the holiday than any other religious denomination. Each Christmas in Moravian communities there was not a single home without a corner set aside for a miniature representation of the events related to the Savior's birth.

Each September Moravian families made a trip to the woods. They dug up great clumps of moss and replanted it in the cool, damp ground of their cellar. A few days before Christmas they would carefully dig it up again and it became the green grass of their *Putz.* Tree stumps were eagerly sought and carried home for the *Putz.* Upside down and draped with moss, the gnarled roots of an old tree created the lifelike impression of a grotto for tiny figures of shepherds and sheep to peer out of, set inside a hill built of real dirt and rocks.

In addition to the little stable scene there was frequently a winding sawdust or sand road, which had to be long enough to accommodate as many as three hundred small wooden animals, which proceeded two by two up the road to a moss-covered promontory on which perched a Noah's ark. The ark and its hand-carved animal passengers were nineteenth-century children's "Sunday toys." While some were made in this country, most were the products of German woodcarvers working in a family cottage industry similar to that of the ornament makers of Lauscha.

Only the most zealous purist could maintain a strictly religious theme in what was basically a children's playtime world. By the 1870s tin soldiers and other secular toys had entered this small world, which for many families became even more elaborate and time-consuming than the Christmas tree itself. Separate areas under the tree were developed with different themes. Spreading outward from the nativity

Late nineteenth-century "skin toys" handmade by German toymakers.

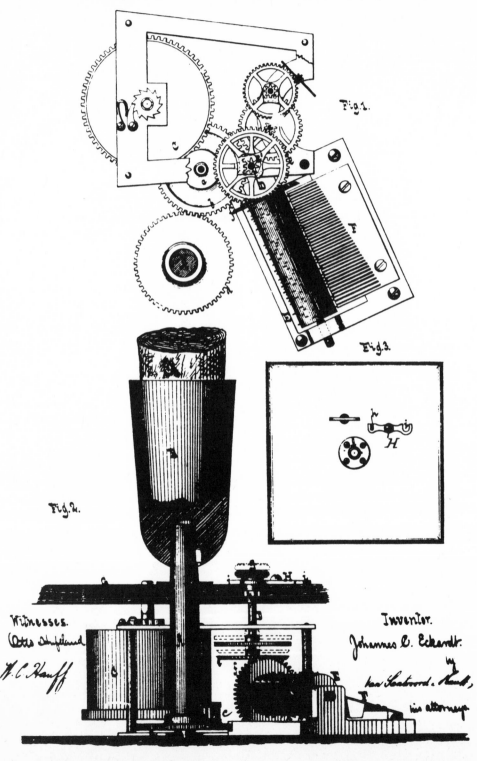

J. C. ECKARDT.
Show-Stands for Christmas Trees, &c.

No. 199,044.   Patented Jan. 8, 1878.

Fig.1.

Fig.3.

Fig.2.

Witnesses.

Inventor.

Johannes C. Eckardt.

his attorney

The patent-application drawing for Johannes Eckardt's revolving musical Christmas tree holder.

OPPOSITE: Late nineteenth-century American Christmas tree stands. The Albrecht stand (right) was patented in 1880, the Merks in 1891.

scene at the base of the tree were other farm or village scenes which, considering the extent of family entertainment in those days, had a way of growing larger and more elaborate every year.

Each Christmas between 1873 and 1876 in Lancaster, Pennsylvania, an anonymous reporter for the *Lancaster Daily Evening Express,* in what was plainly a labor of love, sought out and described in great detail the true-to-nature landscape beneath local Christmas trees. Many had snow- or moss-covered hills, which reached the height of three to five feet; they were made of earth carried indoors by the bushel basketful. Mountains were achieved, in one case, with an estimated half ton of rocks. In some parlor landscapes cisterns temporarily placed in the room above supplied water for streams, cascading waterfalls, and miniature fountains that sent their spray several feet into the air. Cranks, springs, pulleys, water power, and little steam engines drove ingenious clockwork devices, including tiny circular and upright saws in a sawmill; sent a herd of livestock walking across a bridge in a natural procession; gave the illusion of children playing on seesaws, and moved trains and carriages across the hills. Metal goldfish frisked about in one pond as though alive, directed by magnets moving beneath the bottom. Ranged about the two sides of one good-sized room in the home of Frederick Wolf was a succession of eight or nine villages. Houses, churches, barns, shops, and industrial establishments of almost every description, as well as people, horses, and vehicles, were all made from paper. As the *Lancaster* reporter wrote on December 30, 1873: "Days, weeks, yes months, must have been consumed in constructing the villages and other arrangements of this extra-ordinary display."

Emanuel Venter, a tinsmith who had the reputation of having the best *Putz* in Nazareth, Pennsylvania, in the 1880s, had barrels of water stored on the second floor of his home for the purpose of producing waterfalls, brooks, and finally lakes. His barrels had to be filled by hand, so that the water "ran" only while his guests—usually children—were admiring the *Putz*.

By the 1890s, city dwellers could buy artificial moss by the yard or grass-green sawdust by the bag, and also tiny iron fences and trees. Cotton batting and mica crystals represented snow, and pieces of broken mirrors made perfect ice-covered ponds. Toy stores offered entire villages of printed cardboard buildings that could be cut out and glued together. Lead and plaster figurines peopled the streets.

By the beginning of this century families all over America had developed scenes so extensive that it became necessary to take all the furniture out of the parlor, or even both parlors. In one case in Yonkers, New York, the dining room was taken over as well for the duration of Christmas. Many of the realistic miniature objects for these villages were entirely handmade, but a staggering variety of commercially made objects, mostly from Germany, were for sale in this country by 1910.

The high point in Christmas tree landscapes was reached in 1908 when *Scientific American*, the *Popular Mechanics* of the day, gave its handymen readers the printed plans for a Pennsylvania-German-style landscape complete with water-filled streams, a pond, a lake, and a waterfall continually resupplied by means of a miniature "bucket elevator" powered by a small electric motor.

A typical yard contained a large farm complete with houses and a barn and all the outbuildings. Every conceivable barnyard animal was represented in wood, plaster, or celluloid. Among the store-bought animals were little horses and cows, only three inches high, painstak-

A house for a Christmas tree
village made in Japan during the 1930s.

ingly covered by a German toy maker with an animal hide that gave
them the feel and appearance of actual Lilliputian animals. Tiny sheep
wore woolly sheepskins. The complete yard contained a simulated
woods full of hunters and wild animals like deer, moose, rabbits, and
foxes. Over a moss-covered hill would be a grouping of lions, tigers, and
other jungle animals. Realistic scale was never a problem; animals of
disproportionate sizes were easily accommodated in this wonderful
world of imagination. Aeons of time were just as easily accounted for
by another hill, behind which a group of twenty-odd prehistoric
animals roamed.

Time brought steel-spring wind-up trains and alcohol-burning
steam trains that ran round and round the track billowing puffs of
steam, until the little cup of water in the boiler boiled away. Finally
electric trains joined the wonderful miniature world that began as a
simple stable scene at the foot of a nineteenth-century Pennsylvania
farmer's Christmas tree.

In 1901 Joshua Lionel made his first electric trains, and toys that
fathers could give their sons but play with themselves joined the Christmas tree and the Christmas yard as an integral part of the American
holiday season.

A MERRY CHRISTMAS AND HAPPY NEW YEAR.

IX
CHRISTMAS TREES
FOR SALE

 arly each December bundles of some forty million Christmas trees materialize under strings of bare light bulbs on street corners and vacant lots across America.

The story of how trees became a part of the American Christmas is made up of a series of small beginnings. Until the middle of the nineteenth century any family who had a Christmas tree either cut it themselves or ordered it from a farmer. The custom was mostly practiced by first- or second-generation German-Americans, although Americans of other stock had probably begun to hear about the German trees, or had even seen them for themselves, since they are known to have been on sale in Philadelphia markets in 1848.

In 1851, eighty miles north of New York City in the Catskill Mountains on the far side of the Hudson, a man named Mark Carr had the idea of starting that city's first Christmas tree business. Carr knew there were a lot of German families in New York. Since the trees were free for the taking around his home and the cost of transporting them would be his only out-of-pocket expense, he decided he had a good deal to gain and little to lose by trying to sell them.

An old-fashioned Santa Claus strides across the rooftops of New York City in a *Harper's Weekly* engraving of 1869.

OVERLEAF: A Christmas tree market, shown in an engraving from c. 1890.

Carr broached the idea to his family, and although his wife was less than enthusiastic, his sons offered to help him cut the trees. One day in mid-December they loaded two oxsleds with young firs and spruces and drove at a lumbering, slow-motion speed over the rough roads to the Hudson River at the village of Catskill Landing. Here they loaded the trees onto a steamboat, and Mark Carr proceeded alone with them to New York's Washington Market.

Washington Market had been New York's wholesale food and vegetable market for one hundred years. It had been selling a large variety of Christmas greens brought down from the Catskills and over from New Jersey, but until now nobody had thought to sell Christmas trees. (According to a Moore-family story, on December 23, 1822, during a moonlight sleigh ride home from this same Washington Market, where he had gone to buy a turkey, Clement C. Moore conceived the idea for "A Visit from St. Nicholas." He went to his study and wrote the poem, which he read to his six children the following evening.)

A silver dollar secured for Carr the rent of a small strip of sidewalk on the busy corner of Greenwich and Vesey streets, where he set up his trees. What happened was reported in an 1895 article in *New England Magazine*:

Quick and certain was his success, exceeding his fondest expectations. Eagerly customers flocked to purchase the mountain novelties, at what appeared to the unsophisticated country man very exorbitant prices. It did not take long to exhaust the entire stock. And then, highly elated, Mark enjoyed a few days of city life before returning home to gladden the hearts of his boys with the result of their venture and it may be, to crow a little over Dame Carr.

The following year he returned with more trees. That original corner became the center of a burgeoning tree market, which spread outward from the old market until, by the 1880s, with more than six hundred tree dealers competing for space, thirty-some had to rent from the city additional space along the adjacent dockfront.

We do not know exactly how Mark Carr earned his living the other eleven months in the year. *The New York Times* described him as "a jolly woodman," which could have referred to any one of wood-related trades that were the primary industry of the Catskill Mountains.

In those days the area was studded with tiny sawmills and furniture factories, run by water power supplied by mountain streams. Since those streams froze each year from December until March, December was the beginning of a slow season for Mark Carr and his fellow woodmen, so that Christmas trees became an ideal part-time job. Mark Carr remained in the business for many years, and in 1898 one of his sons was still taking trees down to New York.

Seeking an advantage against competition, the men from the Catskills always proclaimed that their trees were the only "fresh-cut" ones. They were quick to insist that trees from Massachusetts or New Hampshire or New York's Adirondacks had to be cut so early that they were drying by the time they got to the New York market. They would grab a branch and shake it vigorously to prove their needles would not fall off. This kind of demonstration was important in the days of wax candles and the ever-present fear of Christmas tree fires. Before many years passed, however, the Catskill Mountain men could supply only a fraction of the trees required by the market each year. Reforestation had not yet been thought of, and it became increasingly difficult to find enough good trees in Rip Van Winkle's mountains. Every succeeding Christmas found the men transporting their trees longer distances from remote parts of the Catskills.

By 1880 a veritable forest of two hundred thousand trees was moving to Washington Market from all over the northeast. They came on boats, by trains, and in big horse-drawn farm wagons, some with a swaying second deck added so they could carry more trees. From about December 10 until Christmas the competition between dealers, and between the dealers and uptown wholesalers who would sell trees to the neighborhood grocers, druggists, and fishmongers, was as sharp as in any of the more established mercantile exchanges of the city.

But not everybody around Washington Market was concerned with making money. On nice December days the tree market was reported to be a favorite spot for loungers. They came to lie around on the soft boughs and inhale the overwhelmingly fragrant balsam scent of the thousands upon thousands of new-cut trees.

The trees were piled up like cord wood in huge piles twice as tall as a man, or they stood on butt ends in long rows for several blocks inland from the waterfront. Sidewalks were walled in behind hills of trees that excluded the sunlight, compelling the storekeepers in adjacent stores to use gas lights even at midday. The merchants were richly rewarded for this annual inconvenience, for by 1870 some were already exacting as much as one hundred dollars for the rental of even a relatively small space for ten days.

Many of the Christmas trees that came down the river on various types of sailing ships stayed on board, where a temporary market was established on deck. Each year a few forty-foot trees rose above the eaves of the ferry house, as tall as the masts of the steamboats and schooners that brought them down the river. The largest trees would soon be found bending under the weight of fruit and presents in the lecture rooms of Sunday schools, missions, and German clubs and societies. The big saloons in the German sections of the city and Brooklyn took most of the twenty-foot trees.

The American Sunday School Society deserves much of the credit for popularizing the Christmas tree. Sunday schools adopted the custom long before most families had trees, and several generations of Americans knew Christmas trees only at church.

Different years saw different styles in trees. Cedar trees were popular in the 1860s, but by 1880 the fashion had switched to evergreens that did not dry as fast and create so great a fire hazard when lighted with candles. A number of old accounts and early photographs of Christmas trees show hemlocks. Their use, however, was relatively small because the ends of their branches were too lacy and frail to support many types of ornamentation adequately.

Up in Maine balsam firs had always been considered a nuisance, because they grew like weeds. A new interest in them for Christmas trees proved very fortunate for hundreds of Maine's rural people as well as for the railroads. The trees' popularity began in 1892, when a steam yacht returning to Boston from Newfoundland called at Sargentville on Penobscot Bay. The beauty of the firs attracted the attention of the owner of the yacht, who took five hundred young trees to Boston and sold them at good prices in Boston's Christmas market at Faneuil Hall. Up to that time pines, cedars, and spruces had been commonly used as Christmas trees, but within a few years of the Boston yachtsman's speculation, balsam became New England's favorite. A decade later about a million and a half trees were shipped annually from Maine.

Men, women, and children worked together in the Christmas tree harvest, and in some localities the cutting of the trees was made the occasion of a general merrymaking, like the husking bees and other farm festivals of the period. The trees were bundled up according to size in lots of six or a dozen and conveyed on hayracks to the railroad station, where they were either sold to traveling buyers or shipped directly to Boston or New York. The farmers got about five cents for each of the smaller trees, ten to fifteen cents for those eight to ten feet tall. In all, Maine people realized about $150,000 a year from their Christmas greens, which was a lot of money for the state in 1900.

By 1893 the demand for trees in New York City finally outstripped the supply and prices were unnaturally high, which created new problems. In 1895 a reporter found a little colony of mountaineers from the Catskills in some confusion over the very important question of selecting a watchman for the night. "Do they steal our trees?" retorted one man in reply to the reporter's question. "Well, now, I should say they do. Just ask Wiltse. He and Fromer have been coming down here for ten years. Do they steal trees? Well, mebbe."

In Washington, D.C., Centre Market, the great food-supply depot, was the place to get a Christmas tree. Throughout the week before Christmas huge wagon loads of evergreens and holly would arrive from Virginia, West Virginia, and Maryland. It was reported that in the 1880s most of the evergreens were offered for sale by country blacks who also sold their own homemade stands. The stand consisted of a large square pine base, around which was erected a picket fence about eight inches high. In the center of the base was a socket for the tree's trunk. The pickets were painted white with red, green or yellow trim. Washington society, which went en masse to the market for their trees, was said to have "fought shy" of these gaudy contrivances, which they said resembled nothing so much as a Southern prison stockade in miniature.

In cities like Washington, Philadelphia, and New York at the turn of this century trees that hadn't been sold by neighborhood grocers and florists on Christmas Eve were never wasted. On Christmas morning the poor would set forth to buy a tree for ten or fifteen cents, although there were those to whom even this was a prohibitive price. They would wait for their tree perhaps until the day after Christmas, or the middle of the week, or even New Year's Day. Mothers told their waiting children that Santa Claus was certainly coming—he had merely been delayed a few days, having so many children to visit, but

163

Right: A Santa Claus candy box.

A detail of a late nineteenth-century ornament made from a chromolithographic print and spun glass.

he would surely come. Finally they would secure a tree, perhaps for five cents. By New Year's Day there was scarcely a tree to be seen.

In the Midwest in the 1880s Christmas trees for cities like Chicago came largely by boat from the forests of Michigan. One family became a legend in Chicago's past as a result of the unique hardships of that trade.

As early as 1887 two brothers named Schuenemann sailed down from Manistique, Michigan, in their fishing schooner with a load of trees they had cut lashed to the deck. They tied up beside Chicago's

Clark Street bridge and began to sell their trees. In 1898 the elder brother, August Schuenemann, with his boatload of trees, was lost in a December storm. (Lake Michigan can be as rough as the ocean in a winter storm.) But year after year the younger brother, Herman, continued to tie up at the same location, and is said to have sold all his trees before anyone else. Everyone who ever met Herman Schuenemann seemed to like him, remember him, and become a regular customer of "The Captain."

One year Herman brought his new bride with him, and the following year and every year thereafter he proudly told his regular customers about his wife and baby daughter, Elsie, and a few years later about his twin daughters, Pearl and Hazel.

In mid-November of 1912 Herman and his crew cut a load of trees in the icy forest outside Manistique and started for Chicago. Like his brother, he too got caught in a Lake Michigan winter storm. His boat, the *Rouse Simmons*, with its crew of seventeen was last seen off Two Rivers, Wisconsin, on November 23. When "The Captain" was reported missing, the Chicago newspapers and the Midwest raised an outcry. Ships were taken off regular runs, private yachts set out, and prominent men persuaded Uncle Sam to lend revenue cutters to join the search. Eventually it became clear the Christmas tree ship would never be seen again.

In 1913 Herman's widow took over his business, and she brought a ship to Chicago each year for many years thereafter. Schuenemann Christmas tree ships were therefore part of Chicago history for forty-seven years.

On the Atlantic coast evergreens for Christmas trees were being cut at a greater rate than ever. Credit for the first Christmas tree farm in the country goes to a New Jersey man named McGalliard. This is his son's account:

In the spring of 1901 my father the late W. V. McGalliard planted some 25,000 Norway Spruce on our homestead farm in Mercer County just outside Trenton. These trees were obtained from Charles Black, a nurseryman in Hightstown, New Jersey, and were, I believe, imported from the Scandinavian countries. Twenty thousand of them were 8 to 14 inch transplants and the remaining 5,000 were seedlings.

Since I was six years of age at the time the event naturally made quite an impression on me. It is my recollection that the trees came packed in moss in a large wooden piano shipping case. They were planted every four feet and cultivated as long as it was feasible.

The circumstances which induced my father to go into this venture are interesting. While I think that Mr. Black, the nurseryman, may have suggested the possibilities originally, the fact that we had a ten acre gravelly field, on which it had become impossible to grow a profitable farm crop, had much to do with it. Noting that a Norway Spruce hedge along the road in front of the farm grew about as well on poor soil as on good, my father put two and two together and figured that Christmas trees might be a good gamble on the ten acres which had been such a problem. The excellent market in Trenton, only four or five miles away, was no small factor also.

When the trees were ready for market in 1907 or 1908, as I recall it, a flat price of one dollar each was established. The customer would make a selection in the field and the tree would be sawed off for him to take along. Many customers preferred to tag their trees weeks in advance for delivery at Christmas. Delivery was made by loading fifty or more trees on a farm wagon drawn by a team of horses and driving the four or five miles into Trenton. The one dollar price was maintained for many years thereafter.

After the original crop was harvested, several other plantings were made by my father and later my brother. All were Norway Spruce, there being no demand for other varieties.

The indiscriminate cutting of forest evergreens for Christmas had been alarming naturalists and conservationists since the 1880s, but suddenly in 1901 America had a conservationist in the White House.

Franklin Pierce introduced a Christmas tree to the Presidential mansion in 1856, and it had become an established tradition by the 1880s. But when reporters asked Theodore Roosevelt how he would decorate his White House Christmas tree, he declared there would be none. Today many think ecology was discovered in the 1960s, but in reality we had just forgotten what a lot of people had known as the twentieth century came in. By 1900 our natural resources had been surprisingly depleted; roughly one-half of all the timber in the United States had been cut. Topsoil was washing away and many of our native birds and mammals were already approaching extinction.

Roosevelt was a conservationist by both instinct and by training. He believed the rate at which we were cutting trees for Christmas alone would eventually destroy our great forests, and so he banned the Christmas tree from his home and urged everyone else to do the same.

Happily for the Roosevelt children, Teddy's sister, "Bannie," had a mind of her own. She gave a Christmas tree party for her nieces and nephews and the whole first family spent Christmas Day at her house. The following year, however, the President was embarrassed to find that two of his boys, Archie and Quentin, had smuggled a tree into the closet in Archie's room.

Teddy described his Christmas and the unexpected breach of conduct in a letter:

Yesterday morning at quarter of seven all the children were up and dressed and began to hammer at the door of their mother's and my room, in which their six stockings, all bulging out with queer angles and rotundities, were hanging from the fireplace. So their mother and I got up, shut the window, lit the fire, taking down the stockings, of course, put on our wrappers, and prepared to admit the children. But first there was a surprise for me, also for their good mother, for Archie had a little Christmas tree of his own, which he had rigged up with the help of one of the carpenters in a big closet; and we all had to look at the tree and each of us got a present off of it.

After a lecture Roosevelt sent the two boys to call on his friend and cabinet member, Gifford Pinchot. Pinchot was the foremost conservationist in the country, and Teddy must have been dumbfounded when, instead of espousing a hard line, Pinchot told them to tell their father that, properly handled, the cutting of Christmas trees could be an asset in helping to thin the timberlands. This was the first of many times Pinchot and the National Forest Service would defend the Christmas tree against its critics.

Officially, the White House continued each Christmas to state that there would be no Presidential tree. However, secretly, Archie was allowed each year thereafter to put up a small tree in his own room. In 1906 a man from New York State, feeling sorry for the Roosevelt children, sent them a Christmas tree, together with a box of ornaments. The gift was summarily returned with a letter stating that the children of the President were not allowed to accept presents from people they did not know.

The frequent pre-Christmas shortage of trees in New York City had become acute by 1905 and in mid-December dealers were reported to be at their wit's end trying to get even seventy percent of their orders filled. Two years later came the worst shortage so far. Sixty-eight thousand fewer trees than usual made their way to the New York market. Editorials and letters urged that only people with children should have trees and wherever possible they should be artificial. (Artificial trees of various sizes had been advertised since at least 1901.) The debate grew fierce. Supporters of Christmas trees pointed out that the best-shaped ones didn't come from the beleaguered forests, but grew along fence lines and in pastures and other open spots, and furthermore, the firs that made the best trees would, if left to grow, never be good for lumber anyway.

In 1909 the Forest Service estimated that five million Christmas trees were cut and that one American family in every four had a tree in its home. Gifford Pinchot continued to say that forest fires and not Christmas tree cutters were the threats that must be checked. He urged reforestation and estimated that the young evergreens then being cut in America for Christmas could all be grown on fifteen hundred acres, if planted four feet apart. He explained that evergreens grow quite rapidly—approximately one foot per year.

But the Christmas tree critics, encouraged by the ever-present shortages, were more vocal every year and they got a lot of editorial support. The *Ladies' Home Journal* in its December 1900 issue gave its readers a decorating idea to replace a Christmas tree. Calling the object a Jacob's Ladder and billing it as an inexpensive substitute, the magazine showed its readers how to cover a stepladder with cheesecloth and greens and candles. Presents were arranged on the steps.

By the 1920s the conservationists were in full voice with a well-organized campaign. The Christmas tree trade finally realized that they were bringing a lot of criticism on themselves by cutting only the trees that were the easiest to get to market. They were buying the rights to evergreens along the roadsides and then felling every tree in sight. Each fall, Americans were exposed to battle-scarred landscapes, and one can hardly blame a 1920s motorist for getting a false impression about what was happening to our forests.

The cutters began to thin rather than to level the trees along the highways, and sound conservation practices became more prevalent.

By 1920 five million Christmas trees were being exported from

Vermont alone. They came mostly from the Green Mountains, where abandoned farms were returning naturally to timber land. (Trees in Vermont forests grow too close together to develop good, full shapes.) Every railroad siding in that part of Vermont was loaded with trees, brought down mostly by horses and wagons, since the winter roads were too bad to be practical for the trucks of that day.

At the same time, Christmas tree cultivation became a profitable business in many parts of the country. Farmers began to find it a good way to use rocky upland pastures and pieces of land not suited to other farming. In the 1930s Franklin D. Roosevelt was the country's best-known Christmas tree farmer. He helped popularize the concept by growing Christmas trees on his estate at Hyde Park, New York.

In the Depression years, a new type of Christmas tree made its debut in America. Scotch-pine farming began as a gleam in the eye of Fred Musser of Indiana, Pennsylvania. Musser was a born salesman—in 1934 he won a national dealer prize selling Chryslers. Six years before, in 1928, he came up with an idea that by 1942 had made him rich and interesting enough to be written up in *Fortune*.

Musser decided that if he planted evergreens on cheap, abandoned, western Pennsylvania farms, he could sell them in five or six years as Christmas trees. Long-needled pines had never been sold as Christmas trees, but Musser believed they could be. He knew that they would be more difficult to decorate than trees with short needles. On the other hand, he pointed out, whereas balsams and spruces start dropping their needles practically the minute they feel the ax, cut Scotch pines will keep their needles almost all winter. Housewives, he argued, would like that enough to offset the difficulty of decorating. And dealers would like it; they could buy early, sell early, and take no loss from dried-out trees. He talked his father, other relatives, and friends into investing in his idea. And he planted his first seedlings.

In 1930 Musser made his first big market test. He cut Scotch pines already on the land, loaded eleven railroad cars, and shipped them all to one dealer in Buffalo, New York, on consignment. He calculated that the trees were worth $1,000 per car wholesale, but got only $198 for all eleven cars. Fred Musser remained undismayed. "We've got a lot more missionary work to do with this product," he told his partners. He continued to ship his pines on consignment, and under his prodding, markets gradually opened up in Chicago, St. Louis, Cleveland, and Philadelphia, though, to this day, New York and New England remain committed to conventional balsams, firs, and spruces.

A blight that attacked millions of balsams in the Maine woods in the 1930s created economic hardship for many in the business and led to importation of Christmas trees from Canada.

In the 1960s the biggest-selling tree in America was the Douglas fir, known in the business as Montana fir. It is an unusually thick, soft, short-needled evergreen. When cut, it holds its short needles longer in our heated homes than other short-needled trees. To supply the demand for long-lasting Douglas firs, Montana suppliers harvest their trees year round and refrigerate them. Cold-storage warehousing also allows Minnesota suppliers to cut trees almost all year long.

Early in the 1970s Fred Musser's long-needled Scotch pine edged out the Douglas fir to become the most popular tree taken home for Christmas. In Nebraska the United States Forest Service and the University of Nebraska are spending hundreds of thousands of dollars in a controlled twenty-year experiment in pursuit of the perfectly shaped, pedigreed Scotch pine.

No matter what the species, or how perfect the shape, or how many millions are sold each year, Christmas trees are still cut and sold, and selected by eager families in a business that Mark Carr could feel pretty much at home with if he were to come back today.

Select Bibliography

The following is a list of the principal books consulted in the writing of this book. To their publishers and authors I acknowledge my debt and gratitude. The list is necessarily short, since remarkably little has been published on the subject of the Christmas tree and its decorations.

Barnett, James H. *The American Christmas.* New York: Macmillan, 1954.

Court, Earl W. *4000 Years of Christmas.* New York: Schuman, 1948.

Evers, Alf. *The Catskills, from Wilderness to Woodstock.* New York: Doubleday, 1972.

Foley, Daniel, J. *The Christmas Tree.* Philadelphia: Chilton, 1960.

Klees, Frederic. *The Pennsylvania Dutch.* New York: Macmillan, 1955.

Lewis, Floyd A. *The Incandescent Light.* New York: Shorewood, 1949.

Riemerschmidt, Ulrich. *Weihnachten.* Hamburg, West Germany: Schroder, 1962.

Robacher, Earl F. *Old Stuff in Up-Country Pennsylvania.* Cranbury, New Jersey: Barnes, 1973.

Shoemaker, Alfred L. *Christmas in Pennsylvania—a Folk-Cultural Study.* Kutztown, Pennsylvania: Pennsylvania Folklore Society, 1959.

Stille, Eva. *Alter Christbaumschmuck.* Nuremberg, West Germany: Carl, 1972.

Winkler, John. *Five and Ten: the Fabulous Life of F. W. Woolworth.* New York: McBride, 1940.

Credits

The author wishes to thank all those who have allowed pictures from their collections to be reproduced in this book.

Page 16 Reproduced By Gracious Permission of Her Majesty, The Queen—Windsor Library, England

Page 10 Staatsbibliothek Preussischer Kulturbesitz, West Berlin

Page 100 Historia-Photo, Germany

Pages 20, 21, 30 The New York Public Library, New York

Page 15 The Leslie Dorsey Collection, New York

Pages 21, 24, 35, 38, 146, 148, 158 The Bettman Archive, New York

Page 6 Collection of Mrs. Charles L. Bybee

Page 48 Courtesy, Henry Francis duPont Winterthur Museum, Joseph Downs Manuscript Collection No. 59x5. 7, Delaware

Page 26 Courtesy, The Henry Francis duPont Winterthur Museum

Page 93 The Smithsonian Institution, Washington

Page 112 Courtesy, Edison National Historic Site, New Jersey

Unless otherwise acknowledged, pictures are from the collection of the author.

Index

Page numbers in italic refer to illustrations.

7' DAKOTA BALSAM FIR   7 ½' DELUXE BALSAM FIR   6 ½' NEW ENGLAND PINE

4' CLIFF PINE